Restaurant Design 2

JUDI RADICE

text by Liz Mechem

The Library of Applied Design

An Imprint of PBC INTERNATIONAL, Inc.

Distributor to the book trade in the United States and Canada:

Rizzoll International Publications, Inc.
300 Park Avenue South
New York, NY 10010

Distributor to the art trade in Canada:

Letraset Canada Limited
555 Alden Road
Markham, Ontario L3R 3L5, Canada

Distributed throughout the rest of the world by:

Hearst Books International
105 Madison Avenue
New York, NY 10016

Library of Congress Cataloging-in-Publication Data
Radice, Judi
    Restaurant design 2 : an international collection
      p.   cm.
    ISBN 0-86636-130-8
    1. Restaurants--Designs and plans. I. Title. II. Title:
Restaurant design two.
NA7855.B47 1990
725'.71--dc20   90-703
                                CIP

*CAVEAT—Information in this text is believed accurate, and will
pose no problem for the student or casual reader. However, the
authors were often constrained by information contained in
signed release forms, information that could have been in error or
not included at all. This refers specifically to the names of hotels,
designers, management companies, architects and
photographers. Any misinformation (or lack of information) in
these areas is the result of failure in these attestations. The
author has done whatever is possible to insure accuracy.*

For information about our audio products, write us at:
Newbridge Book Clubs, 3000 Cindel Drive, Delran, NJ 08370

Color separation, printing and binding by
Toppan Printing Co. (H.K.) Ltd. Hong Kong
Typesetting by TypeLinkPlus
10987654321

ACKNOWLEDGMENTS

As with any project of major proportions,
it takes the collaboration of many talented
people to make it happen. So I must say
thank you to the following people who
contributed time, support and ideas.

To Liz Mechem, a woman of many talents,
who was my partner on this project. To all
of the people I had the chance to inter-
view. To Tracy Davidson whose efforts will
not go unnoticed. To Melissa Pugash, for
her support and fine hospitality.

I am grateful to all the designers, architects and photographers whose spectacular work made this book possible.

Most of all, I would like to thank the staff
at PBC International—especially my editor
Kevin Clark, Richard Liu, Carrie Abel, and
Bedelia Hill whose hard work and dedica-
tion to this project is greatly appreciated.

Judi Radice
San Francisco

DEDICATION

To Beatriz—
You have truly inspired me to appreciate
the natural architecture of life.

TABLE OF CONTENTS

F O R E W O R D

AROUND 1990—PERHAPS A LITTLE EARLIER— we all stopped trying to live up to our blue-and-white china and began to appreciate the homeliness of buffalo china instead.

In regard to restaurants, the change was almost as radical as that. Suddenly, patrons turned against elegance, formal service, luxurious decor and small portions at high prices. They started looking for solid food and better values in bistros, brasseries, cafes, trattorias, grills and establishments that took the hint from the success of these concepts.

Menu offerings at these restaurants consist of homestyle American, lighter California cuisine, authentic ethnic food or, more often than not, a mix of all three. It is no longer extraordinary to find meat loaf on a sophisticated cross-cultural menu and lighter, simpler luncheon foods added to dinner menus in upscale restaurants.

Similarly, cooking methods connected with more casual cuisine have also gained prominence on menus. Smoking, grilling and barbecuing, for example, are popular cooking methods today because they impart flavor without adding fat and because they are folksy and familiar.

As for the guests whose change in taste brought about all these changes in offerings, they are showing up a little earlier for dinner, sometimes wearing blue jeans and often bringing the baby along. It is not uncommon to see patrons in tie and jacket seated alongside patrons in golf shirts. On our side of the table, waiters in tuxedos and starched shirts are becoming much less common and the white apron is in.

What is behind all this casualization? Demographics offer one answer. When the first wave of baby boomers was young working singles, they were eager to experiment with dining out, and new restaurant concepts and ethnic food discoveries abounded. Today, increasing demands are being placed on their incomes as they marry, acquire homes and have children. They have also grown a little older and perhaps more mature. Under those circumstances, it is not surprising that they have lost some of their taste for high-ticket restaurants and are gravitating toward a more casual dining-out experience.

Naturally, this fascination with the casual is also reflected in restaurant design. In the early and mid-eighties, decor was intended to amuse, to dazzle, to raise a

frisson through its novelty. Today the operative words are hospitable, comfortable and accessible. The unifying characteristic of the latest restaurant design is reference to the familiar. Whether you are looking at a retro diner or a modern bistro, you see elements incorporated in order to relax patrons and make them feel at home.

It is not surprising to find knotty pine in an otherwise sleek dining room or mosaic tile and wrought iron railings added to a high-tech interior. In the restaurant of the nineties, we will see a lot of tongue-and-groove panelling intended to remind patrons of the typical family room.

Does that mean that the formal restaurant is gone for good? I don't think so. There will always be a demand for the luxurious, high-ticket establishment in our major cities and, therefore, the restaurant will remain in the frontier of elegant design. But as we move into the nineties, a great number of American restaurants will be showing us how to create the look of taking it easy.

Jeffrey R. Prince
Senior Director
National Restaurant Association

INTRODUCTION

A NEW DECADE BRINGS WITH IT A NEW BUZZ-word for restaurant design: hospitality.

While restaurants in the '80s fairly brimmed over with style, a new formula was beginning to take shape, bringing the focus back to the basics—the food and the service. In this new order, restaurant design has actually gained a more critical role than ever before. As always, design functions as a magnet to bring people into an establishment, but now it must do it-self one better. Restaurant design must keep people coming back, by creating an environment that serves the needs of the operator, while engaging customers with straight-ahead style.

The restaurant design professionals we spoke with, and those whose work is rep-resented in this book, present a unified picture of the direction of design. For all the variation of style, technique and pro-cess, these designers seem to agree that the restaurant of the '90s will be service-oriented.

The '80s saw many trends and styles come and go. Restaurants became theaters, kitchens became stage sets, chefs became celebrities, and the general public became connoisseurs. At best, these develop-ments offered a dazzling alternative to the traditional dining experience. At worst, the restaurant of the '80s served high de-sign at high prices, sometimes at the ex-pense of the food and the service.

Chicago architect Bill Aumiller, principal of Aumiller Youngquist, P.C. calls his three-point formula for success "the food-service-design triumvirate." Adam Tihany, a New York-based restaurant designer has a similar list of critical factors: "value, accessibility, style and substance." Both designers provide for the needs of the customer by placing an equal emphasis on the back of the house and the front of the house.

Designing for smooth operations and flow of service is now seen as a crucial factor for success. Tihany requires each member of his design team to work one day a month in Remi, a restaurant he co-owns, to provide them with first-hand operations experience. Without a well-orchestrated service plan, says Tihany, the restaurateur will face obstacles to success: "they will lose help," he explains, "and that will af-fect the operations of the restaurant." Ultimately, design serves the customer by serving the operator.

Keeping their restaurant interiors on a "human scale" is a primary concern for many of the designers represented in these pages. Comfortable seating, inven-tive ceiling treatments, carefully planned lighting and control of noise levels all con-tribute to an atmosphere that is people-oriented. These factors can make the difference between a restaurant that is effectively a stage set, and one that is a setting for service.

A changing clientele may lie at the heart of these changing attitudes. An easy dem-ographic formula tells us that as the baby-boom generation ages, and has less money and time to spend on leisure and enter-tainment, value and quality become pri-mary concerns. This translates to people eating out more and wanting to spend less. While this may ultimately lead toward more casual restaurants taking precedence, it also means that customers are more so-phisticated as a whole, as dining out is no longer the special-occasion exception but the daily norm.

With this newly sophisticated customer base in mind, many designers are seizing the opportunity to express more complex ideas in their work. Cultural and ethnic in-fluences can be mixed to create new schools of design; Michael Guthrie, a principal of San Francisco-based Guthrie-Friedlander Architects calls his firm's approach to design a "collage of elements, rather than a homogeneous single concept." Futuristic French, Pan-Pacific, 21st-century Deco and a "nuts & bolts" brewery are just some of the design concepts that capture the imagination of designer and customer alike.

Entertainment is still a premium in restaurant design. For some designers, like Northern California architect Ron Nunn, the entertainment in a restaurant comes from "the conversation at the dinner table." For others, like Los Angeles restaurant designer Barbara Lazaroff, it takes the form of an exhibition kitchen, which engages diners in a kind of "participatory theater." Of course, an imaginative, beautifully executed interior is still a critical factor in the success of a restaurant. Whether it's a grand-scale operation or a small, personal project, creativity sells.

The notion of the restaurant as theater has evolved since it burst on the scene some tens years ago, with the popularity of the exhibition kitchen and the theme restaurant. Just as styles vary within the theater itself—from minimalist Beckett to ornate Baroque, styles vary on the restaurant stage. Some designers follow a terse

script, in which the minimum of design detail is used to express an idea; others are effusive in their visual dialogue, layering concepts and design elements.

Most designers agree that the exhibition kitchen is here to stay; as Lazaroff points out, "the exhibition kitchen has always been popular; it has its roots in Europe, and has existed in America for years in the form of diners and drugstores." The newly interpreted exhibition kitchen in the fine dining establishment provides entertainment, warmth and what Lazaroff calls "a sense of connectedness to the food we eat." This colorful stage for food preparation poses design challenges of lighting, stylistic integration and service flow.

Creating a unified image, in which architecture, interior, graphic and lighting design all work together, is a common goal of most of the designers represented in these pages. Successfully integrating all these design elements is seen as critical to establishing an identity for a restaurant. Designers now consider no detail too large—the exterior of the building, or too small—the matches and business cards, to demand their full consideration. For Monsoon in San Francisco, architect Mark Mack constructed an eye-catching, bright yellow structure to flag the restau-

rant's entrance. Other designers choose exterior treatments appropriate to the style of the restaurant inside.

This new attention to detail extends to the tabletop, as in the case of Michael Graves' design for Palio in the Walt Disney World Swan Hotel, or even to the bathrooms—Noa Noa and Paradise, both in Los Angeles are notable for their racy restrooms. A final detail that can neatly tie up the whole concept is the restaurant's name, signaling an esthetic shared by the food and the design.

The restaurants represented in this book are notable for their understanding of principals governing restaurant design today. They are original, beautifully executed and, most importantly, they work. To provide a better understanding of the process behind the finished product, each restaurant is presented along with information about the challenges each designer faced, and their creative solutions. Rough sketches, diagrams, before and after photographs and sources of inspiration are helpful in understanding the scope of each project. The proof of the process lies with a satisfied customer, who responds to good looks, professional service and outstanding food. Bill Aumiller sums it up: "Restaurant design is the balance of functionality and esthetics."

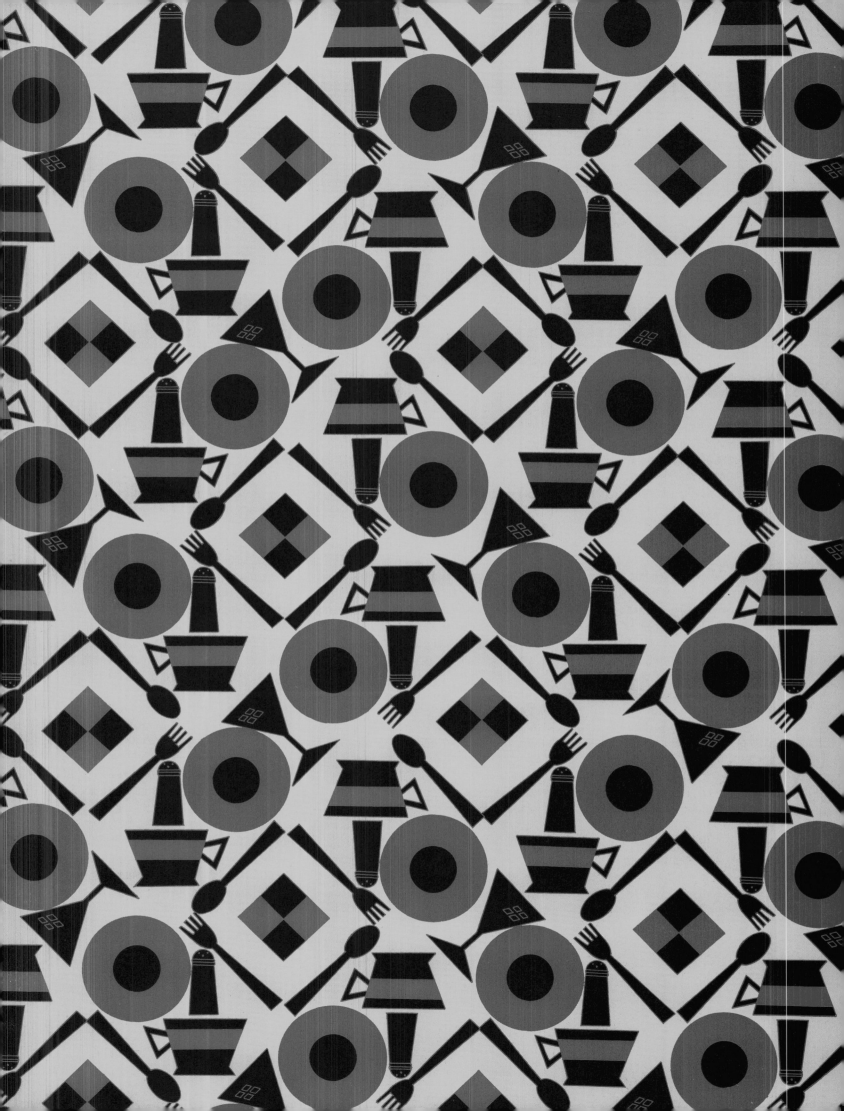

INTERVIEWS

Aumiller Youngquist, P.C.

Bill Aumiller and Keith Youngquist
Aumiller Youngquist, P.C.
Chicago, IL

Bill Aumiller and Keith Youngquist are the principles of Aumiller Youngquist, P.C., a Chicago architecture and interior design firm. Among their many award-winning restaurants are the "timeworn" Italian dinner spot, Scoozi, the subtly funky Mexican eatery, Hatdance, the Spanish tapas bar, Cafe Ba-ba-Reeba and the stylish American bistro, The Eccentric, which boasts a large and colorful exhibition kitchen. The partners often work with Lettuce Entertain You, Inc. to create some of the most remarkable dining experiences in Chicago. Their most recent interior design award is from Restaurants and Institutions magazine, for their Tucci Milan project in Chicago. Aumiller and Youngquist were themselves judges for the 1990 R/HDI awards.

Q: With a string of successful restaurants to your credit, what are your thoughts on your design approach?

A/Y: It's become fairly commonly accepted now that there are three major factors that make a restaurant a success, and one of them is the design. The other is service, and of course the quality of food. Most restaurants really have to have all three going for them in order to be successful. The design can give people the reason to initially come to a place, but if the service or the food falls short once or twice, it doesn't matter how pretty it is; they're not going to keep coming back.

Q: On the other hand, what do you think are the most overlooked aspects of restaurant design?

A/Y: Lighting. Lighting is very definitely one of the major factors that gets overlooked. It can make or break the restaurant design from an esthetic standpoint. You need to make sure that the general lighting is done so that the customer and food are presented in the best possible light. Then pick out the accent lights and spotlights so you emphasize focal points within the room. You also have to think about distracting attention away from areas that you don't really want people to concentrate on. Ideally, lighting acts as both a decorative and a functional element.

Q: How do you deal with the front of the house and the back of house?

A/Y: Well, that's the next point. In addition to lighting, operations become neglected by a lot of designers, either because they overlook it, or because they don't really understand it. When this happens, they build in roadblocks and areas of conflict within a space—not providing proper service stations, not planning for traffic patterns, so that functionally it may look right, but that second portion of the design-service-food triumvirate is falling short.

Q: What happens when the kitchen is in itself a stage, as in The Eccentric?

A/Y: In the last 10 years, as display kitchens became much more popular, it got to the stage where people were exposing kitchens just because it was the trend. We tell our clients, fine let's expose the kitchen, but let's have a reason for doing so and let's have a means for controlling it. Quite frankly, a kitchen isn't something you want to show every hour of the day. We have big curtains at The Eccentric that can be opened, so the "actors" can be put on stage any time, or the curtains can be closed during busy times like a lunch rush.

Q: What about bathrooms—can you have fun with bathrooms?

A/Y: Oh, sure. At Scoozi the women's bathrooms are all individual compartments with a water closet and sink. You can have fun with the layouts or with the fixtures. We put statues of David in the women's washrooms at Zarrosta. It's definitely another aspect of restaurant design that could afford to be showcased a little more.

Q: How do you deal with the integration of graphics in your design projects?

A/Y: What we're after is integrating everything into the overall impact of the restaurant, so it makes a major statement, rather than a series of disjointed statements. That carries through to the graphics—the menu design, the logo. We hire a graphic designer early in the project, and try to conceptualize everything in the beginning stages. Our specialty is architecture and design, not graphics, so we really value the graphic designer's ideas. We do give input, of course, because we usually have a hunch as to whether a logo is going to work on letterheads and matchbooks and also be effective when it's enlarged on the outside of a restaurant.

In terms of exterior signage, we like to think of the whole building as a sign. Like the Red Tomato—it has a very distinctive mosaic tile pattern that in itself becomes a sign. The actual sign is only about two feet square, but it doesn't seem to hurt the restaurant's popularity; the place is always packed from opening to closing.

Q: Could you discuss the idea of the concept restaurant?

A/Y: What we think is more important than following the latest trends is really making a concept statement. Whatever the concept is—be it an Italian farmhouse, a '50s diner or an Italian sculptor's studio, to really zero in on it and use whatever materials are available to make that overall statement. Usually the client comes to us with a basic food concept, and then we try to determine what will make this project unique, give it its own history and personality. A good example is Tucci Bennuch. The concept is aimed at overcoming the cold, kinetic atmosphere of a shopping mall, to create an Italian country farmhouse feel. People can feel that they've found a haven away from the hustle and bustle. The warmth of the design reiterates this concept.

Early on in any project, we'll sit down and brainstorm with the creative team—the owner and hopefully the chef too, even the different artists and the construction crew, and come up with a real narrative statement that defines exactly what the *experience* of the new place will be. That's the concept. Knowing your direction from the food to the design to the overall esthetic statement. It's like setting up a new business each time you open a restaurant.

Q: Is there a difference between a concept restaurant and a theme restaurant?

A/Y: Absolutely. A concept restaurant can be a theme restaurant, and often is. The problem is that there are a lot of theme restaurants that have no concept.

Q: Do you think food courts will be a major trend in the '90s?

A/Y: One of the problems with food courts is that people are looking for a haven from the shopping crunch, and I don't think food courts really provide that. They're more an extension of the mall itself, not a separate environment. It's also very hard to make an image statement when you're little more than a storefront. You're trying to fit a microconcept into something much larger that usually has no concept. Unless you make a concept food court, like a village marketplace that's full of food stalls, then you have an idea for everyone to build on, rather than a disunity for everyone to overcome.

Q: How do you meet the different design challenges offered by renovation vs. ground-up construction?

A/Y: We have the most fun with renovation. The existing architecture makes it more challenging, particularly if the space hasn't been a restaurant. For example, Scoozi was a rust-proofing garage, and The Eccentric was a parking garage. The trick is to take what seem like limitations, turn them around and make them work for you. There are some beautiful old spaces that have a certain architectural character to them which will really lend itself to a new restaurant. Ground-up construction is almost too easy; it's less of a challenge.

Q: Could you discuss your use of computers in the design and presentation process?

A/Y: We used to use a lot of renderings and models, but they became lengthy, time consuming and not really that effective. We now have a pretty complex computer system, an autocad and a datacad. Through the process of 3D imaging, you can get a pretty good idea of the interior of a space. You can't see the finishes on the walls, but spatial relationships become very apparent. We try to really use the computer as a design tool.

Q: Will restaurant-as-theater continue into the next decade?

A/Y: Definitely. The clientele has become much more sophisticated over the last ten years, and really demands a higher quality of space. People go out to eat more now, as they cut back in other areas like travel. Restaurants are a quick fix of entertainment. And it's a communal thing, like in Italy where you meet friends and really socialize. We're becoming more Europeanized in that respect.

We're also interested in more social or communicative forms of eating, where people don't just want to see and be seen in a pretty space, but also want to really talk with the people across the table from them. Certain types of cuisine lend themselves to this, like Spanish *tapas*, or some Asian dishes. Sharing food from a common pot or actually participating in its preparation seems to generate excitement and communication between customers.

Q: How did you come to specialize in restaurant design?

A/Y: It's very fulfilling from a design standpoint, to be working on an Italian trattoria one day, a French bistro the next, and a '50s diner the day after. But more than that, there's real gratification in seeing your designs in action. In other forms of design, you know whether or not you're happy with the final results, but you may never know if the user is happy. With restaurants, you know. If the public isn't satisfied with the design, they won't frequent the place, and it will go out of business. Restaurant design is the balance of functionality and esthetics.

Brantner Design Associates

Cheryl Brantner
Los Angeles, CA

Cheryl Brantner, a designer based in Los Angeles, approaches her work from an interdisciplinary perspective. Her many years of formal apprenticeship to several noted architects have given her an architectural orientation, but she practices interior design and graphic design as well. Brantner's best known restaurant project, Patina, which opened in Los Angeles in 1989, brings together her many talents for a finished product that has been featured in Metropolis, Vogue *and* Esquire.
Brantner has been involved in restaurant design for the last decade. Her background in political science (she describes herself as a former '60s activist) and her experience as a craftsperson have given her a discerning, intellectual approach to the field. She is currently at work on a new restaurant for chef John Sedlar—Bikini, which will open in Santa Monica in early 1991. She describes the food as "pan-cultural" and the design as "urban riviera, with more emphasis on the urban part."

Q: Your approach to restaurant design can be characterized as interdisciplinary. Please explain how you come to a project, and the various hats you wear in the course of its completion.

C.B.: So often people get categorized as being an architect, graphic designer, interior designer or product designer, but I don't think I fit into any one of those slots. I don't classify myself as an architect, although my background is architectural, and that has given my design work a particular slant. I really like to think of myself as just a designer. In the case of Patina, I even found myself contracting out the work and being involved in the down and dirty process of getting it built.

Q: How do you make a presentation to a client—do you sell yourself as an all-around designer with a total concept?

C.B.: I've been lucky with my clients that I am able to really have a lot of input into the concept, and I'm often left to my own devices. Sometimes it's hard for people who aren't trained in the design field to read plans and visualize things three-dimensionally. So the clients are sometimes surprised when, seven or eight weeks into the construction process, shapes start to take form and they say, "oh, so that's what it's going to look like!" Restaurants really are like the theater in that way—it all comes together at the last minute.

Q: Are the concepts based more on food or set design?

C.B.: It often has to do with the food; chefs who come to their second or third restaurant are often eager to experiment with different types of cuisine. In the case of Patina, the concept, that of a progressive European look, really came from the client, Joachim Splichal. His phrase was "France in the '90s," and it fits with his cuisine, which is

based in the classic French style, but incorporates the best aspects of California. We talked about it a lot, and he was really focused on the name, which he envisioned as the beautiful finish that comes from silver that ages over the years. The restaurant was being built on the site of Le Saint Germain—the oldest French restaurant in Los Angeles, so that added meaning to the concept, that this space had its own patina of age.

I resisted the name at first, because the word "patina" has become associated with the design trend of faux finishes, which is now almost a cliché. But I saw that architecturally I could push the concept a step further, with my own take on the idea. I always bring a certain amount of philosophy and theory to what I do.

Q: What is behind your theory and philosophy?

C.B.: It depends so much on the client and what the space and project are going to be. Patterns and shapes and textures usually begin to grow as I start the schematic design. Something speaks to you in a slightly skewed way, and that's the hint that a philosophy is emerging. For Patina, I defined the concept as a layer of information, that acquired a certain truth and beauty and value over usage. So we tried to give the walls layers of detail and history. I think in any design, there's a certain built-in set of values or ideas that the public never sees, but it governs your design process.

Q: How do you integrate architectural elements with the graphic design of a restaurant?

C.B.: They should be very closely linked. Often the client doesn't think of putting the money into it—menus can be quite expensive, but the graphic elements are a real lasting memento. The architecture should definitely be coordinated with the graphics. In my case, it's often not even deliberate, because I'm designing both elements, so my eye kind of unifies them. The logo I designed for Patina has a direct relationship to the architecture; it's all upper case, serifed, very extended custom type. Under that, there are nine bars, which look like vertical stripes. It was intended that those stripes would create a kind of square with the type, and also represent a classical moulding type of relief. On the menu, the logo is embossed, so you literally have the relief in repetition. Architecturally, that thin vertical element is incorporated very subtly in just about every room. Although only about one out of a thousand people will notice it, it was deliberate. The spirit of the design prevails.

Q: Do you treat the exterior signage with the same attention to detail?

C.B.: I would never just put the logo etched or painted onto a flat surface and then just attached to the building. To me, exterior signage should be like sculpture. It has to work in a third dimension and perform its function, which is to identify the place. Hopefully, it can do all that in 18 square inches or under. I'm opposed to the concept of big signs or billboards to draw your attention to a restaurant.

Q: Where do you draw the line between the exterior and interior design?

C.B.: I don't think there should be a line. There has to be a direct connection, even out onto the sidewalk. If you have the option to design the exterior, it should be very abstract and eye-catching, and yet within the sphere of the rest of the project. And it should be functional—I don't believe something should be there just for esthetic purposes. At Patina, the space is divided into four little rooms,

each with a front window onto a little patio. In front of each of these is a very large stell trellis; seen together, they appear to march along the sidewalk. The trellises serve several purposes—as sculptural elements and as functional elements which support the planting, as well as acting as a visual and sound barrier between the street and the restaurant. And from inside, they introduce a wonderful degree of privacy to each of the rooms. For Patina, there's really no drawing the line between the interior and the exterior—it's all interrelated.

Q: How do you use color in your designs?

C.B.: Color, or the consideration of it, is really essential. At Patina, there's no color, and that's deliberate. I chose a neutral pallette to let the materials retain their natural qualities. The various woods we used were left with their own irregular characteristics, as was the steel and glass. The fabrics are all very neutral—they are sumptuous and beautiful, but not loud and splashy. This way the textures speak, the shadows speak and the lighting speaks.

Q: Where does your inspiration come from?

C.B.: Much of it comes from my travels. I always keep a visual diary, which I go over with my staff members periodically. So when I see the way a shadow falls across something, that may later determine how I'll design a doorjamb. Or when I see a certain color, I think it will make a great stain for a wood wall. It's really just in the way you look at things, a certain way of seeing, so that going to a museum or taking a walk in a funky part of town will later translate into a design solution. The real beauty lies in taking things out of context, superimposing them on some other idea or element, and coming up with an esthetic that's entirely new.

Q: What do you think makes a restaurant successful?

C.B.: There are so many factors that go into it, that it's hard to separate them. Certainly design is a key factor, but there are really two different kinds of restaurants. There are those wonderful, purely indigenous ones, whose success is mostly food-related, and there's very little design involved. Places like Versailles, in Culver City, which is a strange little place in an unhip part of town, but the food is great, so there are lines every night of the week. Every city has places like that. Then there are places that are consciously designed, where the ambience is such a big part of the venue. In those cases, the food really has to measure up, or the restaurant won't succeed, and the management must know about operations. Perhaps two out of three of those elements can keep it going for awhile, but ultimately, it has to all work together.

Q: What do you think is ahead for restaurant design?

C.B.: I don't see how we can keep going with the big-scale restaurants. Those have really topped out, although I think we can keep doing what we're doing in creating exciting, innovative interiors. The economy will probably have much to do with it. I'm really drawn to some of these little cafés that have been cropping up all over Los Angeles in the last year or so—little bohemian, art-student cafés, like Java. They're not consciously designed, although there is always an inherent sense of style evident. The furniture is sort of a hodge-podge of '40s and '50s stuff, but you find you have the best conversations in these little places, sometimes more so than in the big star see-and-be-seen restaurants. Maybe it comes back to why we really like to eat out to begin with—to feel some sense of community. Ultimately, the people involved in any process are what's most gratifying about it.

D'Amico + Partners

Richard D'Amico
D'Amico + Partners, Inc.
Minneapolis, MN

As President and Founder of D'Amico + Partners, Inc., Richard D'Amico brings a fresh and innovative approach to the midwestern restaurant scene. Along with his brother Larry, who is executive chef of the Minneapolis restaurant design and management company, D'Amico has established himself as a leader in the field. The brothers' stylish D'Amico Cucina, which opened in 1987, won rave reviews as a "world-class restaurant." They followed in 1990 with the dynamic Azur, Inc., a complex of three restaurants in downtown Minneapolis' Gaviidae Common. The flagship restaurant, Azur, presents rustic Mediterranean French cuisine in a witty, avant-garde setting.

Since D'Amico + Partners was founded in 1983, it has grown to national recognition and its projects have received numerous awards. The firm is currently at work on their first bar/nightclub which will open this winter.

Q: What is your design philosophy at D'Amico + Partners?

R.D.: We are a risk-taking, creative company when it comes to design, but we have a very conservative approach when it comes to business. There are so many components that go into making an operation successful, that you can't ignore any of them. All those elements like graphics, food service, setting, lights — the more you really look at each one and try to hit the nail on the head, the better chance you have at success. When someone enters a restaurant for the first time, these components all work together subliminally to create an overall impression, so initially, each one is as important as the other. Once you get going, the thing that keeps people coming back is the food.

Q: How do you approach a new project?

R.D.: After we look at the architecture and the basic space planning, I develop the style. I always start by thinking how I want people to feel in the restaurant — not so much what they'll see, but what the mood of the place will be. Then I look at different furniture styles, the color palette, finishes, textures. I try to go out and find or design elements that will match what I'm thinking about in terms of the esthetic sensibility. My inspiration often comes from viewing a lot of movies, especially from the '30s and '40s. Some newer films have been a source of inspiration too, like *"Bladerunner"* and *"Batman."* It's like set design in a sense — you're designing sets for people to be entertained while they're eating.

Q: Describe the relationship between the food and the design in your restaurants.

R.D.: One asset we have as a company is that we're operators and chefs as well as designers, so we know what it takes to make a restaurant happen. My brother Larry, who is executive chef, and Steve Davidson, who is a partner and manages all front-of-the-house operations work with me as a team on the total concept. In the case of D'Amico Cucina, the food and the design really come from the same source — the space has the feeling of a very comfortable Tuscan villa, and the food carries that through.

With Azur, the style of food that we do is almost the opposite of what the design says. The food is very rustic — French Mediterranean peasant dishes, and the design is anything but rustic. We didn't start off by trying to incorporate these contrasts, but in thinking of a new French restaurant, we wanted to avoid the typical pitfall of being too stuffy. So there are no tablecloths, the music is a mix of French rock & roll and the food doesn't come from the *haute cuisine* tradition. It all really works together to generate excitement.

Q: What were some of the design considerations with the Azur project?

R.D.: The facility is located on the fifth floor of a vertical mall in downtown Minneapolis, right at the epicenter of the business district. Saks Fifth Avenue is the key retailer in the mall, taking up four floors.

Azur, Inc. actually is three different restaurants—Azur itself is a full service restaurant, and is really the star of the show. Then there's the Azur Ballroom, which acts as an alternative to the typical hotel ballroom, geared toward business meetings, receptions, celebrations. And Toulouse is a casual kind of brasserie, with takeout food and seating, which is targeted to downtown shoppers, office workers and the people who work in the mall.

Another consideration, frankly, is the weather. If you're familiar with downtown Minneapolis, you know that it's a tough market, because there's no year-round street activity. In the summer, people are everywhere, but as soon as it starts to get cold, all the foot traffic moves to the skyway level. We knew that once we got people up to the fifth floor, the look of the place would draw them in, but the only way to get them up there would be to take some risks design-wise. We needed to create something that people would talk about, and would return to with their friends.

Q: What does taking risks mean to you?

R.D.: I think you have to take risks with design. Anything that is really good, really high-quality does. If you don't take the risk, you take the low road, and you'll end up with something that's been done before. You just hope that you're doing it in the right place and at the right time. Because no matter how much research you do, no matter how many books you read or people you talk to, there's

nothing that's going to tell you if a project will work. There's always an element of luck that comes in. You hope that your timing is on the mark. If you're lucky, you're right. If you're unlucky, you struggle. Or if you're ahead of the game, too progressive, you may struggle until things catch up.

Q: Your restaurants have a very strong graphic appeal. How do you incorporate graphics into your planning and design?

R.D.: Graphics, and the logo in particular, are so important because often they're what the public sees before they see anything else. It's a critical investment, and we like to bring the graphic designer in at the very beginning, after we know what the design and service concept will be. We've been working with Duffy Design Group, and are always pleased with what they do. Usually I make a list of all the collateral materials we'll need, from sales brochures to menus to matches to wine list. I'll outline what the criteria requirements are—what the use and design orientation will be for each piece. They take it from there and come back with something wonderful.

Q: How do you view the integration of architecture/interior design with the graphics?

R.D.: We talk about that with the graphic design firm. It often happens if we're on the same wavelength. For example, the metal menus for the Azur project complement the perforated metal we use in Toulouse—these little panels that separate the tables; we affectionately call them "confessionals."

Q: In terms of planning, what do you think are some of the most overlooked aspects of restaurant design?

R.D.: It's easy to forget what a beating a restaurant takes. I've seen some places that have been open only two years, and they look ten years old. Wear and tear and stress on the facility is a really important consideration in the initial design. Also, the designer must consider how adaptable it will be to change. Hopefully you've created somethat that's relatively timeless, that's not so trendy that it will be dated right away. You don't want people to come in and say, "oh, remember how everyone was doing that style three years ago," like all the fern bars we had in the '70s. You hope the restaurant won't fall into such a definable niche that it will have to change drastically just to keep up.

Q: What is ahead in the next decade for restaurant design?

R.D.: In general, I think there is a definite **long**-term trend toward more casual restaurants, places that people can go to often and **feel** comfortable in. It has to do with price **value** and quality, and not needing to be too dressed up. People are eating out more and will want to spend less. My own future plans are to just continue taking as many risks as I can and hope that we're doing something fresh and different. Then maybe people will leave talking not only about the food service, but about the experience overall.

Imaginings Interior Design

Barbara Lazaroff
Imaginings Interior Design
Los Angeles, CA

Los Angeles-based Architectural Interior Designer Barbara Lazaroff brings an individual flair and theatrical imagination to restaurant design. Lazaroff is widely credited as one of the originators of the exhibition kitchen, which she introduced with the highly acclaimed Spago over ten years ago. Along with her husband Wolfgang Puck, Lazaroff owns and operates Spago and the popular Chinois on Main, an eclectic take on Chinese cuisine. Most recently, Lazaroff opened Eureka Restaurant and Brewery, which incorporates industrial elements for a stunning and original effect.

Lazaroff has gained international recognition for her innovative work in the United States and Japan; she has been the subject of numerous magazine articles, and has often lectured on restaurant design and maintenance. She is currently at work on the Mediterranean inspired Granita, which will open in Spring 1991 in Malibu.

Q: What are the most important considerations in restaurant design?

B.L.: The food and the people are the stars of the space, and a restaurant must be designed with this sense of purpose. Just as a museum is specifically designed to showcase art in the most functional and aesthetic manner, a fine restaurant is designed for efficient and skillful food preparation, and people must feel comfortable and stimulated dining there. I feel it is a mistake to build a restaurant where the focus is not primarily on food. My restaurants are chef-oriented. I devote forty-five percent of the floor space to the kitchen alone. If the chef and the people who work there every day do not feel comfortable in their own space, they will never be able to produce the kind of food that makes the customer feel comfortable.

Q: What makes a restaurant work?

B.L.: Although publicity is very important, when I think about what makes a restaurant work, what makes it successful, I am not just talking about the first year and whether it gets written up in the local newspapers or in *W* and gets on the covers of the design magazines. Success, to me, is ongoing longevity for the restaurant. The staying power is what we must look at. To achieve that you must provide for the staff, and you must think about location, placing your restaurant in a neighborhood which relates to it, where there is

mutual support between you and the community. At Spago, for example, only twenty percent of the customer base is comprised of those celebrities which get all the press. The rest is made up of neighborhood people, or people who just feel comfortable in the space. The wonderful thing about that is that you can come there in a sweater or in "black tie" and sit down next to a mailman or a movie star. It's this breakdown of socio-economic, racial and class barriers which give Spago a sense of animation, energy, and realness, and that helps make it successful.

Value is also extremely important. It is imperative that people feel they are getting their money's worth. They may resent the space if they feel they are paying for the wall treatment. You may build the most spectacular place, but if the food isn't any good and the prices are not moderate, people won't come back. They may bring their friends by to look at the fabulous space, but they won't want to pay for more than a glass of wine. Then the tables will be empty and the restaurant may have difficulty sustaining itself.

Now that's the restaurateur side of me talking! And that person is in constant battle with the restaurant designer side of me. I am always thinking about how to make the restaurant innovative and exciting, as well as functional.

Q: Why do you think the exhibition kitchen has become so popular?

B.L.: In some ways, it has always been popular. This is not a new concept; it has existed in America for years and years...we have the diner, the drugstore. In Europe, particularly in the South of France and Italy, you have wood-burning ovens right in the dining room. It was perceived as a new idea when we put an exposed kitchen in a fine dining establishment, which we did with Spago over ten years ago. That was very avant-garde then and it tended to demystify the food preparation process. This gives people a sense of connection to the food they eat, which is so lacking in an urban community. It also offers a sense of spectacle, of drama, of diners being in some kind of participatory theatre. You're a part of the play!

While exhibition kitchens have this sense of spectacle, they also have a sense of *haimishness* about them...that's a Yiddish word which means homey, down-to-earth. People are stimulated by having the kitchen in the dining room, but they are comforted by it, too. The sounds, the smells, the memories...the kitchen is the hearth of any home, and it's the heart of a restaurant. It's what pumps life into it. You have the sense of built-in warmth and familiarity from an exposed kitchen.

Q: What are some of the problems posed by an exposed kitchen?

B.L.: Noise level and lighting are the most critical. Really, the lighting is so problematic. In some restaurants, the lights in the rest of the dining room may be just fine, or even wonderful, but the lighting in the exposed kitchen is just atrocious. Or when they try to make the lighting scheme attractive, they forget the functional needs of the kitchen, and wind up creating visual hot-spots for the chef and lighting from behind so that the staff can't properly see what they are doing. There is a real dual challenge in lighting an open kitchen.

Q: At Eureka Restaurant & Brewery, your customers are treated to a view of the inner working of the Brewery. What was the thought process behind this?

B.L.: It is our concept of a brewery in the '90s. It is very neo-industrial; a play on *"Metropolis"* and Charlie Chaplin's *"Modern Times."* When most people think of a brewery, they think of dark wood, a very European, Dark Ages kind of concept. But I had an ingenuous conception of what a brewery might be: all the equipment, the huge gears, rivets, moving parts. So, I played upon that, and went with a very mechanized, cybernetic feeling. There are 7,000 nuts and bolts, in stainless steel and polished brass. All the materials play into this theme: hand-hammered and polished copper, brushed stainless steel, perforated pewter. It sounds very cold, but it is actually quite a warm, appealing space, done on a very human scale.

When we started work on Eureka, the function of the project was our departing point. It is a restaurant, connected to a brewery where we brew beer for national and potentially international distribution. I considered how I could utilize the visual impact of the enormous brew kettles, and decided to let the brewing operation take center stage. The kettles are viewed as one approaches the building, and from the interior as well. It is the same concept as the exposed kitchen: the customers are participating in this process.

Q: What is the status of your current work-in-progress, Granita?

B.L.: Granita is really the antithesis of Eureka. Granita is on the ocean, near the Malibu Colony, so the design inspiration is the water and the natural elements. I thought of the sea as the "source that we all come from": that primordial soup. I envision the space as a three-dimensional watercolor, and the palette subdued with some textural surprises and biomorphic forms. It's very fluid in form and uniquely utilizes the quality of light that Southern California is famous for.

Q: How do you deal with graphics in your overall design scheme?

B.L.: I think they are so important. They should tie into the theme of your restaurant; it is an emblem that can make a strong statement about the feeling of your restaurant. Actually for Chinois on Main, I did the logo before I did the restaurant design. I extrapolated that *yin-yang* sign and the painterly feelings of the letters to almost every surface in the space. Undulating door and window mullions, as well as a serpentine bar top, and unusual curved tubular-shaped soffits.

Although I have completed the design work for Granita, this is the first time I have conceptualized but not completed the logo before moving into the construction phase.

The graphics for Eureka posed additional responsibilities. Because the logo would appear on our beer bottles, a product which would be sold in the marketplace, we felt the graphics had to have the best impact for store display and for product identification. Barbara Eadie of Bright & Associates was the designer who created the Eureka graphics. This was a selection process of ten or twelve designers all

working simultaneously on different ideas. We felt Ms. Eadie's was the most elegant and strongest visually. We started with a product, a very high-quality beer made with the finest ingredients and brewing equipment available, and felt the logo and label design had to spell that out. It was a design decision that took a full year.

Q: How does your creative process work?

B.L.: I can actually visualize the restaurant before I begin work on it. Down to the light fixtures, where the art is, what I would like the finished product to look like, or especially feel like. I even see people dining in the space. It is this whole esoteric thing about the feeling of the restaurant. After I think about it for a few weeks and come up with all these ideas, I lay out the footprints of the building first and see how much space we have. Then I start by laying out the kitchen; this is where Wolfgang or the chef of the restaurant is critical in terms of input. Next, I mark out where the front door will be, how I want people to enter the space, and try to arrange it so that most people can see the kitchen from their tables. Then, once we get all the functional planning out of the way, electrical, mechanical, I get to go *crazy*. Every single element in the restaurant gets my full attention. Nothing goes untouched, or at least unconsidered, and the lighting design is paramount.

Q: What are your ultimate goals with restaurant design?

B.L.: I love an element of surprise. We talk about continuity, but for me, continuity includes contrasts. It makes a space so exciting, just like the people who come there who are all so different from one another. I like people to be moved, by giving them an element of magic and fantasy. I want to stimulate their intellect, and I want to provide an environment where people can relax and feel comfortable. That is a precarious balance, and that is where my challenge lies.

Ron Nunn Associates

Ron Nunn
Ron Nunn Associates, Inc.
Tiburon, CA

Ron Nunn is an architect based in Tiburon, CA and the Napa Valley, in California's wine country. He brings 25 years' experience to his straightforward restaurant designs, which are some of the most popular and acclaimed in Northern California. For eight years, Nunn was a partner and board member of San Francisco's Spectrum Foods, and designed many projects for them, including Ciao, Prego Ristorante and Tutto Bene.
Nunn frequently collaborates with his wife, Hannah, an interior designer. Some of their most recent projects include the award-winning Lark Creek Inn in Larkspur, CA, Bistro Roti in San Francisco and a series of Piatti restaurants which originated in the Napa Valley and have now opened in several Southern California locations.

Q: How do you deal with graphics and interior art in your projects?

R.N.: It's usually a joint decision with the client. We make recommendations on people we've worked with before, and have had great success with interior art in particular. In Piatti, for example, we've just been making some changes involving graphics. We hired Evans & Brown to come in and do some work in the interior, to replace the revolving art exhibitions we had been installing through the Museum of Modern Art in San Francisco. The new graphics are very whimsical, tongue-in-cheek, and all having to do with food. At the doorway, there are two huge asparagus spears that form columns.

Tutto Bene is another good example of interior graphics making a big statement. Originally the space was really big and cavernous. The key goal was to break it down to a more human scale, so we ended up with these three big sections. It definitely called for some major mural work. The artist, Ann Field came in and picked right up on the colors we had already chosen; she just did a great job with that graphic mural.

Q: Do you approach a restaurant's design differently if you know there will be multiple units?

R.N.: No, I don't. In fact, Piatti is a good example of that. When we had completed the first one in Yountville, and were beginning work on the second one, which was in Santa Barbara, everyone involved sat down to decide if we wanted to do a different look. We all voted against it, and went with the same tile floor, the same basic design elements. The formula works well in Yountville, and we wanted to carry that through; the people will come there and will like it for the food, they'll feel comfortable there. The only thing we consider, of course, is the building it's going into; that can change the whole look. The new one in La Jolla is a little cottage right off the beach. It will have low ceilings and be a very tight three or four separate rooms, whereas Yountville is one big room with a high ceiling.

Q: Do you have any preferences for spatial treatment in your restaurants?

R.N.: I really believe in having a tight space, not having great big areas. The tighter the better, even with the aisle space. It may mean that the waiters will have to edge through with the tray, but I think it contributes to a feeling of intimacy. If a space is too big, we'll try to squeeze it down just by using walls and furniture. Keeping things on the human scale is so important.

Q: What is your view of the restaurant-as-theater approach?

R.N.: I do think many people go to restaurants for theater, but there are so many ways to define that. It's really just an evening event, and the drama can come from the people, from an open kitchen, or even from the food itself. A restaurant that looks like a knockout set design can be theater the first time you go to a place, but after that, it comes from conversation with the people you came with, or seeing friends across the room who call to you to come over to their table. I don't think someone's going to holler across the room for you to come see their light fixture. A good example would be Jeremiah Tower's Stars; there's so much life and activity that just comes from his kitchen. That interest, combined with the great food, is…what keeps people coming back.

Q: What's ahead for restaurant design in the '90s?

R.N.: The fun, small-scale restaurant will be the direction of the next decade—informal places, sidewalk cafés. I think we're really going back to the classics, back to the little European-style restaurant, where all you need is a nice clean white tablecloth, some wine glasses, a candle and some great food. No gimmicks, lots of staying power. Stick with the classics, and, like those little places in Italy, you'll have a restaurant that will be there forever.

Q: How would you describe the Ron Nunn approach? Your style could easily be called minimalist.

R.N.: The words I use are clean, crisp, functional and light feeling. I feel very strongly that it's the people and the food that make the restaurant, not the design. We've all been guilty of super-design, but I think people

are getting burned out on it. To me, successful restaurant design is no gimmicks. Some of our biggest projects, like Bistro Roti, are really straightforward. I don't think any amount of interesting materials, textures, wall finishes or handwoven fabric will give the same amount of animation and activity as the staff, the customers and the food itself.

Q: What is your most representative restaurant?

R.N.: I used to think it was Ciao in San Francisco—for many years that really exemplified my style. Clean white walls, really effective in letting the people take center stage. In fact, I remember when Ciao opened in 1979, critics were skeptical; it was accused of being too sterile, like an operating room. But on opening night, it was a real showplace for people, for what they had on, and for their personalities. And eleven years later, it's still an immensely popular place.

My choice now for a favorite restaurant would be Piatti. It's the closest to what our philosophy is—really a people place. The original one, which we opened in Yountville in the Napa Valley has such a simple design, using basic materials. We used a floor of old Mexican 12″ tiles, off-white stucco walls, a basic timber chair we sourced out of Idaho, and one fabric color. And when I look back now on how low the budget was, and that we came in under budget, it's really hard to believe. But people keep coming back. You look around on any given night and see not just the Napa Valley tourists, but people from the wineries, all the locals—I'd say that's success.

Q: How much of a consideration is the budget on your projects?

R.N.: Bringing in a project within budget is a number one factor for success. If a restaurant is over budget and under-capitalized, you'll see it go under quickly. Actually, it's more of a challenge to do it with a smaller budget and be successful, to get the most effect for your dollar. It doesn't excite me for someone to say, you have five million dollars to do this all-out restaurant. If someone comes to me and says let's do two little 180-seaters, I've got a limited budget, but I'm a great chef, I'm more excited about those projects than anything else.

Q: Do you prefer working on renovations or projects that start from ground zero?

R.N.: Being an architect, I can do either, but I get just as much fun out of doing renovations. Actually, dealing with new construction can be such a long process, with city and federal codes. You can save a great deal of time and expense by going in to an existing restaurant and turning it around quickly. It just means getting in there, spending time in the space, and seeing what you can do with it, what you can change and what's valuable about it that you want to keep—again, always with the budget in mind.

Mike Quon Design

Mike Quon
Mike Quon Design Office
New York City

Mike Quon is a New York graphic designer and illustrator who often works in the restaurant design field. One of his most noteworthy projects is the award-winning Minters, a take-out deli designed by Tony Chi/Albert Chen & Associates in the new food court/atrium of Manhattan's World Financial Center. Minters was judged Best Quick Service Facility by R/HDI in 1989, and was highly praised for its "fantastic graphics."

Q: Could you speak about the importance of graphic design within the restaurant design field?

M.Q.: Graphic design in general is responsible for conveying information, adding vitality and establishing a sensibility for the restaurant. I like to think that graphics, in the form of signage, logos and menus, add life and pizzazz to a project, and help to convey the image. In fact, graphic design has really become a top priority today in the restaurant field, just as it has in the business world. For example, logos are extremely important in today's competitive market; we've all become very sophisticated in the common visual language. The architect who understands the value of this will pull in a graphic designer quite early in the project.

Q: In the original planning stages?

M.Q.: Ideally, yes. We like to think that we're not just decorating a surface, but that we are concept people, thinkers too. Often the graphic designer has good instincts and hunches on what's right for a project that can benefit the entire design team. Sometimes we lack the ability to think in three dimensions, which isn't that important when you're just talking about logos. But the design disciplines are crossing over all the previously set barriers these days. Graphics are integrated into sculptural shapes, or echoed in the interior design. The more closely we work with the architect in the beginning stages, the more unified the final project will look.

Q: How was the Minters project initially presented to you?

M.Q.: When Tony Chi first told me about it, I was really excited to be working on a project with such high visibility. He showed me rough sketches of the food court, which was unlike any food court I'd ever seen. I was really amazed at the whole high-end feeling of it—very elegant.

Q: What were your design solutions for the project?

M.Q.: I saw that there was going to be a lot of glass in the atrium, so I created a logo you could see through. I also used my experience as an illustrator to create these very loose drawings that are silkscreened onto glass, images like ice-cream cones, fruits, baked goods. These were placed next to the logotype, which itself was kept quite small. This immediately gave the signage an elegant, higher tone; it didn't scream out, but it visually communicated information and an image. The takeout menu had a slightly different approach—the logotype was larger, but we kept the illustrations, which were really appropriate for Minters' multi-lingual, multi-cultural audience.

We carried the theme of the illustrations and the checkered border through the different elements—three different size ice-cream cups, napkins, counter cutouts, drink cups and aprons that acted as uniforms. Of course, the menu board was key. Once again, the illustrations really paid off; even if someone couldn't speak or read English, if they saw this big ice cream cone, it could act as an icon, and they could see that this was the section for ice cream.

Q: What are the design challenges posed by a food court?

M.Q.: Well, of course, you want to do the best for your client so that their space really stands out, but you also want to keep a basic sensibility so that all the establishments work together as a whole. You can sense the right tone, and strike a compromise. In the case of the World Financial Center, it wasn't really that difficult, because most of the other clients were fairly upscale, quality operations that understood the importance of good design.

A second consideration with food courts is maintaining great attention to detail in very small spaces, so that you can immediately communicate a theme or a complete concept. The graphics have a lot to do with the success of a food court establishment.

Q: Looking forward into the next decade, what do you expect to be some major trends in restaurant design?

M.Q.: I think the food court is going to be a very big-time trend of the next decade. There will be more focus on quality fast food in an unusual type of setting, including good value. It's extremely competitive out there. Some restaurants are even cutting back their prices. And, as we eat out that much more, we have to take the cost into consideration.

The food court serves several needs, because it provides value, and also appeals to the American view of free choice. Everyone can get what they want in a food court—one person can have a hamburger, another can have Mexican food. Also, the economic reality of today dictates lower prices and more selection for the customer. The food court is a competitive market within a larger competitive market, so I think we will see a lot of quality developing there.

Q: How does that fit in with large scale, theme restaurants?

M.Q.: Of course, the two can easily coexist. People go to restaurants for different reasons. That's why we have really elegant French places for the romantic dinner, and then we have the boisterous, trendy places. Hopefully, you can combine good food with both.

Q: What makes a restaurant work?

M.Q.: Even if you have all the best ideas and people working on a project, the timing can be off, and you fail to attract the right crowd. Then you're left with this beautiful space that just sits empty. Ultimately, people make the place. But a lot of it is trial and error—there's no perfect formula every time. Good instincts are hard to quantify.

Q: What are some common obstacles to success?

M.Q.: I think it has to do with the kitchen and the layout—the way the place flows, or doesn't flow. If the traffic patterns aren't carefully considered, it can cause a lot of problems. Another thing that new restaurants sometimes do is aim too high, overshoot their mark. You have to be very realistic about what you can handle.

Q: What's ahead for the graphic designer in the restaurant design field?

M.Q.: We just have to keep doing a great job on those menus and logos, because people are really watching that. It's what they take home with them. The graphic elements are the fine little accents that tell people that a restaurant really has tied it all together. Graphics help to complete the experience down to the smallest detail.

Adam D. Tihany International

Adam Tihany
Adam D. Tihany International
New York City

Adam Tihany, principal of the New York-based Adam D. Tihany International, is widely considered one of the foremost restaurant designers in the United States. Some of his best known projects include Bice, Huberts, La Coupole, Remi, Le Cirque and Metro, all in New York, as well as Biba in Boston and Bice in Beverly Hills. With the opening of Remi in New York in 1987 and in Santa Monica in 1989, Tihany became an owner/operator as well as a designer. Current projects include the opening of new Bice restaurants in Paris and Miami, and Primi Piatti in Washington D.C.
Tihany's 17 years in the field have made him a keen observer and authority. In addition to his restaurant and hotel design work, he has designed two separate lines of furniture and has completed extensive work for private residences. Tihany is a featured judge in many design competitions, he lectures frequently on restaurant design, and teaches a course on the subject at New York's School of Visual Arts.

Q: How has the restaurant design field developed during your long career?

A.T.: First I should say that restaurant design as we know it didn't really come into being until about ten years ago, when people started to recognize that restaurants aren't just places to eat; they're places to come and be entertained and to see people. We began to break out of the old clichés of restaurant design then — the typical expectations that if you went to an Italian restaurant, there would be checkered tablecloths, Chianti bottles and salami hanging off the ceiling. The difference lies in the changing habits of dining out. Most people go to restaurants because they want to show off a little, learn something, have an experience. So, for this selective and sophisticated new clientele, you're required to provide something that serves their needs.

Q: What is your basic philosophy of restaurant design?

A.T.: I am a firm believer in the concept of hospitality. The basic premise of the restaurant, the root of the word itself, is a place that restores someone's life. It is a place where you come to rest, to eat, to get taken care of, and leave hopefully with a smile on your face, not sweating, hassled and with an empty pocket. I respect people too much to focus just on the spectacle. For me, a spectacular experience is when you leave happy and you get what you've paid for. You can sum it up with four words: style, substance, value and accessibility.

Q: How do you incorporate this credo into your design work?

A.T.: Well, comfort is always a major consideration. Very simple elements like noise level, lighting, comfortable chairs, enough space to move around in, the color pallette you choose. These are considerations no matter what type of restaurant I am designing.

Q: You have worked on a wide variety of projects in your career; what is the hallmark of a Tihany restaurant?

A.T.: I don't think there is a trademark to my restaurants. Putting my individual stamp on it isn't my main concern. My main concern as a designer is for the customer to have a consistent experience from the moment they walk in, until the moment they leave. The food, the service, the attitude must all be coherent.

There's a famous saying that you can't sell atmosphere. Well, if you can't sell it, you can certainly control it. When you walk into a restaurant, the first thing you see is someone greeting you at the door. Their look and attitude can establish your whole image of a place, which must carry through to the design of the restaurant and the food that is served. If you walk into a place and the maitre d' is wearing an elegant tuxedo, everything is extremely formal, with polished brass and wood everywhere, soft classical music playing, and he leads you to table with beautiful appointments, you sit down, and they put in front of you a hamburger and french fries on a brown plate, you say, "wait a minute, something's wrong." You must unify all these elements.

In addition, the design of the restaurant must be right for the client. If someone hires you to give them a new image, it's like getting a new suit, and they must be comfortable in it. You can't give a Jean-Paul Gaultier suit to someone who has always worn a tuxedo. They're going to feel uncomfortable, and they won't be able to run their operation the way they want to. So if your restaurant design is like a suit that is tailored to fit the operator, and if they're someone you respect and like to work with, then you have it made. My trademark is maybe a satisfied client, more than an instantly recognizable design.

Q: How do you incorporate graphics into your overall restaurant design?

A.T.: Graphic design usually comes in right after the concept development stage, which comes from a collaboration between the client and me. Sometimes the graphics have to do with a particular aspect of the restaurant, or they become part of the decor. In Remi, for example the name actually means "oars" in Italian, and that's the departing concept for the style of the restaurant. We carry the Venetian theme all the way through, with a drunken gondolier sliding down an oar. In the case of Biba, which I think is very strong graphically, the graphics are really an expression of the temperament of the owner, Lydia Shire. Her soul really comes through—painted on the walls and ceilings. This is where graphic design can personify the establishment.

Q: Please discuss the course you teach in restaurant design at the School of Visual Arts.

A.T.: It's wonderful to see that people from so many design disciplines are interested in the subject—interior designers, graphic designers, chefs, restaurant managers. It's now taken seriously as a subject for the curriculum. Basically what I do is I design a project from A to Z with the students. I'm the client; I tell them what kind of restaurant I want, and they have to come up with a marketing study, a location, the name—all of it. I invite experts to come and speak on different aspects of the business, from kitchen design to graphics. Often the students start off thinking restaurant design is just an exercise in interior design, but in the end they come away seeing all the elements it takes to make it work.

Q: What are the most overlooked aspects of restaurant design?

A.T.: The biggest problems are service and flow. In my office, I have a policy that each designer has to work at least one day a month in my restaurant, Remi, in any capacity. This way they can see what it takes to make service function properly. Care must be taken for the people who work in a restaurant every day, not just for the people who visit there. The needs of the operator are being grossly overlooked with inefficient design, if they keep losing help and can't develop a good crew. They get taken in by this magic word—design. There's a lot of wear and tear in daily use that designers so often aren't aware of. We can make a place look sensational, but making it beautiful is a question of makeup, not design.

Q: How do you design differently for multiple unit restaurants, as in the case of Bice, which has locations in several cities?

A.T.: It's quite fascinating to see how each restaurant adapts to its location. Each one is quite different, but in keeping with the Bice style—a new kind of trattoria that has none of the clichés of a typical Italian restaurant. I don't think there's a universal concept that works everywhere, except perhaps for the Hard Rock Cafe, which has identified its clientele. I'm a great believer in a really good local partner who you respect, who understands the concept and knows their market. Otherwise, it's very difficult to go from one headquarters to different locations around the country, and still provide personal and personable service.

Q: What's ahead for restaurant design in the next decade?

A.T.: I see the restaurants of the '90s as being simple and uncomplicated to understand, not overly intellectual. They serve clean healthy food that you could eat three or four times a week. It's not necessarily an event to go to them. They're based more on reality than on fantasy, and are designed to the human scale. Of course, all of that must be done with great style.

PROJECTS

The Ace Cafe

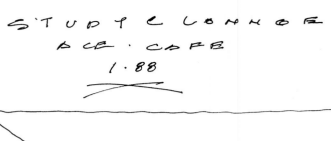

THE ACE CAFE IS PROOF POSITIVE THAT a lot of imagination can prevail over a little budget. Created on a shoestring, this small restaurant in San Francisco's hip South-of-Market area has become one of the city's most popular new eateries. Architect Robert Bernardin came up with design solutions for the long narrow space that perfectly suited the owners' goals. "We wanted to use materials with intrinsic value, avoid faux finishes and address the industrial nature of the original space," explain the "Ace boys." Bernardin started by reinforcing the room with ceiling beams and two rows of columns, one of which delineates the kitchen and bar. These functional modifications became an integral part of the interior design.

"A new realism" is what Bernardin calls the clever, utilitarian style he developed for the Ace. The furniture, which he designed and contracted work on, relates to the architectural detail through its use of common materials and finishes; the imaginative chairs, tables, bar stools and streamlined torchières are all constructed of warmly-stained maple, steel and glass. The cafe's name was borrowed from the infamous hangout of the '50s and '60s "Rocker" motorcycle scene in England, and reflects the owners' interest in vintage British bikes. "Besides," say the Ace boys, "it sounded right."

Architecture/Interior Design
Robert Bernardin
Proprietors
Adam Fisher, Courtney Persinger, Jr., William Stone
Photography
Donna Kempner

Type
Informal Cafe
Size
1,500 sq. ft.
Seating
60
Opened
1988
Budget
$82,000, complete with furnishings and appliances

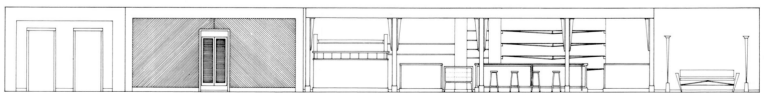

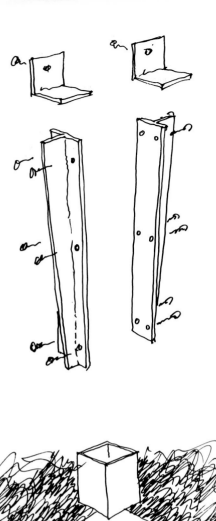

TORPEDOS
ACE · CAFE

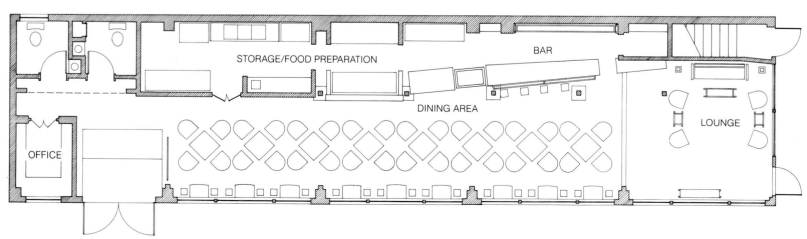

OFFICE

STORAGE/FOOD PREPARATION

BAR

DINING AREA

LOUNGE

Andiamo!

ART, FOOD AND WINE TAKE CENTER stage in Andiamo!, the dramatically spare, museum-like restaurant designed by John Harding in the Bel Canto building in New York's Lincoln Center area. The contemporary art collection of owner Lewis Futterman is displayed with a minimum of extraneous design elements. Harding left the two-story-L-shaped space at the rear of the building windowless; natural light is let in through three skylights punched out in the ceiling, which are covered with translucent fabric to control the amount of light and to filter out harmful sun rays that might damage the artwork.

The soaring, 30-foot ceilings and an abundance of hard surfaces presented an acoustical challenge; Harding chose a sprayed-on wall finish in a matte-white tone to absorb sound and add texture and interest to the interior. Decorative floor-to-ceiling columns, some of which are actually exhaust pipes from the basement-level kitchen, define the space vertically. Low matte-black chairs and a bold, tubular black stairway add weight and width. The stairway, constructed as a series of "platforms in space" serves a functional and esthetic role. "We wanted to create some excitement for people sitting in the mezzanine, and to draw the eye upwards," says Harding. Each turn of the platform offers a new perspective of a piece of sculpture or a small painting, giving these pieces of art a place of importance.

Architecture/Interior Design
John Harding Architect
Proprietors
Lewis Futterman, Francis Crispo, Terrance Singleton
Interior Artwork
Lewis Futterman Collection
Photography
Scott Frances

Type
Full Service Restaurant/Art Gallery
Size
2600 sq. ft., dining area; 1700 sq. ft., kitchen
Seating
100, dining room; 45, mezzanine; 10, bar
Opened
1988

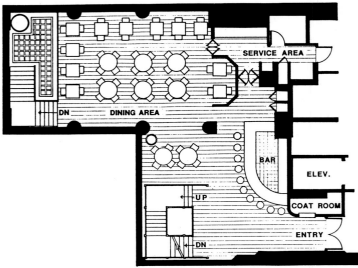

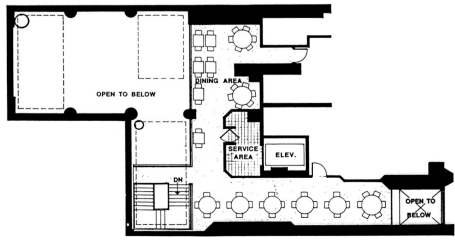

Angelica Kitchen

ANGELICA KITCHEN SERVES "CRE-
ative macrobiotic" food in a
homey dining room on Manhattan's Lower East Side. Architect
Larry Bogdanow's challenge was to move
the 15-year old restaurant "into larger,
brighter surroundings, and not to lose
their loyal following." Bogdanow worked
within a modest budget to create an environment that was "friendly and accessible, and not too slick," as his client
Leslie McEachern requested.

The interior of the restaurant was in need
of some repairs when Bogdanow took on
the project. Crumbling walls were treated
with joint compound and many layers of
paint to play up their roughness and character. The finished look is warm and Mediterranean. Bogdanow steered clear of too
much color, allowing the natural wood
tones of the furniture and exposed beams
to define the restaurant's character. Deep
blue tiling used for the floor of the open
kitchen is continued into the dining room
in a grid pattern. The color is picked up
in the wall sconces, which were constructed of blue glass bowls resting on
wrought-iron plant stands, for a remarkable $25 each.

Architecture/Interior Design
L. Bogdanow & Associates Architects;
Larry Bogdanow, principal
Proprietor
Leslie McEachern
Photography
Daniel Eifert

Type
Macrobiotic Restaurant/Bakery
Size
2,300 square feet
Seating
60
Opened
1989
Budget
$132,500

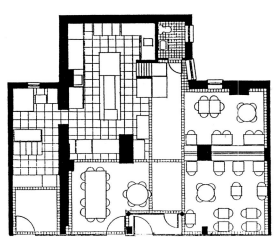

Atlas Bar & Grill

LOS ANGELES, CA

ARTIST RON MEYERS' SPECTACULAR design for Atlas Bar & Grill transformed a cavernous space into a setting that evokes the magic of mythology. Restaurateur Mario Tamayo presented Meyers with the name he had selected, and left the rest of it up to the designer. Meyers' take on the Atlas concept used Greek mythology as a departure point, with stylistic references to the Art Deco period. "In trying to recapture the glamour of the 1930s, I took the point of view of a designer in the 21st century looking back into time," says the designer. He consciously avoided literal Deco influences, and focused instead on "historical connotations."

To appeal to a broad audience, Meyers says he dealt in universals for his design choices. Figures of gods and goddesses from Greek mythology are the subject of overscaled wrought-iron screens that surround the main dining area. Budget constraints didn't allow Meyers to drop the ceiling, so he painted the exposed pipes a deep blue; the room's overhead scale is lowered with suspended lightning bolts, hung with crystal pendants to reflect light from the starburst light fixtures. The smiling gilt sunbursts are actually closet doors that are used to store sound equipment for Atlas' weekend live entertainment. Acoustics in the large room were softened by cork floor tiles and heavy curtains hung in the front of the restaurant. A gold piano near the sometime stage area lends a fanciful touch of luxe.

Architecture/Interior Design
Ron Meyers
Proprietor
Mario Tamayo
Photography
Tim Street-Porter

Type
Global Cuisine/Nightspot
Size
3,700 square feet
Opened
1990
Budget
$250,000

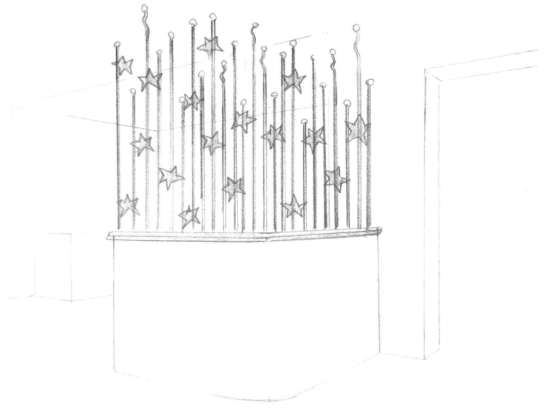

Azur

ONE LOOK AT AZUR DISPELS ALL preconceptions of the French restaurant. Sleek metal, marble and wood replace white tablecloths, rock & roll replaces classical strings, neon replaces candlelight and Garlic Soup Provençal replaces the standard French Onion. The star player of the three-restaurant Azur, Inc. complex in Minneapolis' Gaviidae Common, this startling new space is the brainchild of Richard D'Amico, president and founder of D'Amico + Partners. In a deliberate juxtaposition of moods, the futuristically designed restaurant serves rustic peasant cuisine created by Richard's brother, Larry, executive chef of D'Amico + Partners.

D'Amico says of his plans for Azur that he "wanted to avoid being too stuffy — the typical pitfall of the French restaurant." Instead, he allowed influences like *The Jetsons, Bladerunner* and *Batman* to inform his bold esthetic, which even carries though to the bathrooms. "You have to take risks with design," he says, "or wind up with something that's been done before." Named for the Côte d'Azur on the French Riviera, the restaurant's interior makes liberal use of the shade of blue the region is famous for. Curving, biomorphic shapes, skillful lighting and innovative materials contribute to Azur's animated, electric feeling. Original graphics by the Duffy Design Group complete the avant-garde image.

Architecture
Shea Architects; Gregory Rothweiler, project manager
Restaurant Design
D'Amico + Partners, Inc., Richard D'Amico, principal in charge of design
Proprietor
D'Amico + Partners, Inc.
Graphic Design
Duffy Design Group
Photography
Christian Korab

Type
French Mediterranean
Size
20,000 square feet (entire complex: Azur, Azur Ballroom, Toulouse)
Seating
120 (Azur alone)
Opened
1990

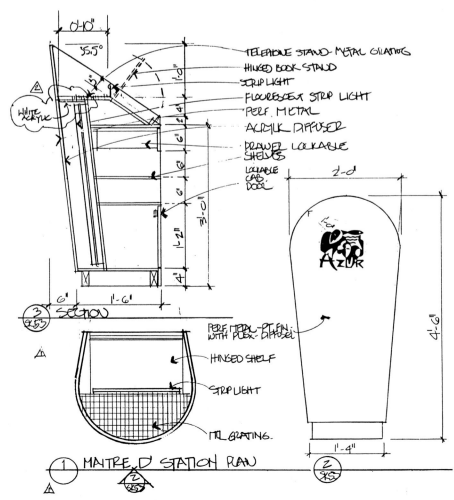

TELEPHONE STAND-METAL GRATING
HINGED BOOK STAND
STRIP LIGHT
FLOURESCENT STRIP LIGHT
PERF. METAL
ACRYLIC DIFFUSER
DRAWER LOCKABLE SHELVES
LOCKABLE CAB. DOOR

WHITE ACRYLIC

0-10"
35.5°

3'-0"

6"   1'-6"

③ SECTION
95'3

PERF. METAL-PT.FIN.
WITH PLEX. DIFFUSER
HINGED SHELF
STRIP LIGHT
MTL GRATING.

① MAITRE 'D STATION PLAN

2-0

4'-6"

1'-4"

②
85'

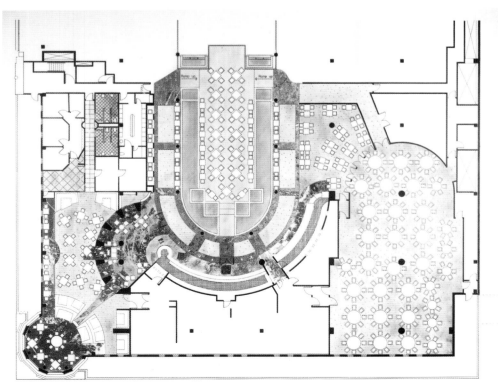

Biba

"THIS IS LYDIA'S PERSONALITY YOU see painted on these walls," says designer Adam Tihany of the vibrant interior he created for Lydia Shire's lively Boston restaurant. The space is comprised of two stories, connected by a staircase that features a curving, Gaudi-esque metal balustrade and red lacquered handrails. A street-level bar welcomes guests to the interior, which is painted a rich, mottled gold. A mural by Robert Jessup enlivens the lounge area with its depiction of reveling people, farm animals and a bounty of food. Throughout the space, Tihany has used warm tones of gold, red and green. The low ceilings are painted with bold geometric patterns that are reminiscent of Albanian kilim rug motifs. Forest green and maize upholstery fabric used in the lounge, with its stylized animals and trees, takes its inspiration from Diego Giacometti. The dining room floor is diagonally striped blond and brown cherry maple, while the bar and lounge have a natural terracotta tile floor. "Biba is a restaurant with incredible soul," says Tihany. "But it's not mine, it's Lydia's. I was just the hand that pushed the pencil."

Architecture/Interior Design
Adam D. Tihany International
Proprietor/Chef
Lydia Shire
Graphic Design
Adam D. Tihany, Monica Banks
Mural
Robert Jessup
Photography
Peter Paige

Type
Full Service, Eclectic American
Size
1,900 sq. ft. main dining area; 2,618 sq. ft. upstairs dining
Seating
50 main dining area; 150 upstairs
Opened
1989

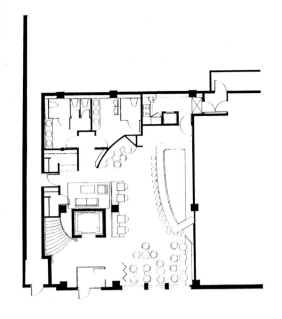

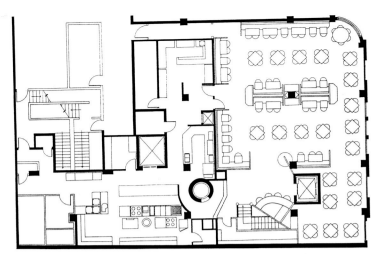

Bice

THE RUGGIERI FAMILY'S FAMOUS BICE restaurant has operated in Milan for over 60 years, and serves as loose inspiration for the several U.S. restaurants of the same name. Roberto Ruggieri's primary concern was to make the environment of his new world establishments palatable to the American sense of style. Restaurant designer Adam Tihany responded with a gorgeous solution, a style he calls "a new kind of trattoria, that is very Italian with none of the clichés." The polished wood, clean lines and artful lighting fixtures speak to an American conception of Italy as a center of design—"we think today of Armani and Ferrari, not checkered tablecloths and bottles of Chianti," says Tihany.

There are now Bice restaurants in New York, Beverly Hills, Chicago, Washington, D.C. and Miami, and a Bice in progress in Paris. In designing for multiple units, Tihany says "it's quite fascinating to see how each restaurant adapts to its location; each one is different, yet each one keeps the Bice style." The polished wooden surfaces and curved chairs travel from one restaurant to the next. Bice in Beverly Hills gets a spectacular ceiling treatment which is equal parts traditional Tuscany and twentieth century. This stylish family of restaurants does justice to the Bice name.

Architecture/Interior Design
Adam D. Tihany International
Proprietor
Roberto Ruggieri
Photography
NY: Karl Francetic/LA: Toshi Yoshimi

Type
Northern Italian
Size
NY: 3,078 sq. ft., one floor
LA: 2,061 sq. ft., main floor; 3488 sq. ft., upstairs
Seating
NY: 142, restaurant; 28, private dining; 30, bar
LA: 160, restaurant; 205 private dining upstairs
Opened
NY: 1987/LA: 1989

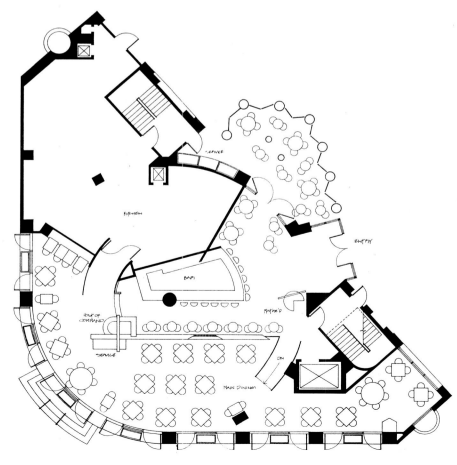

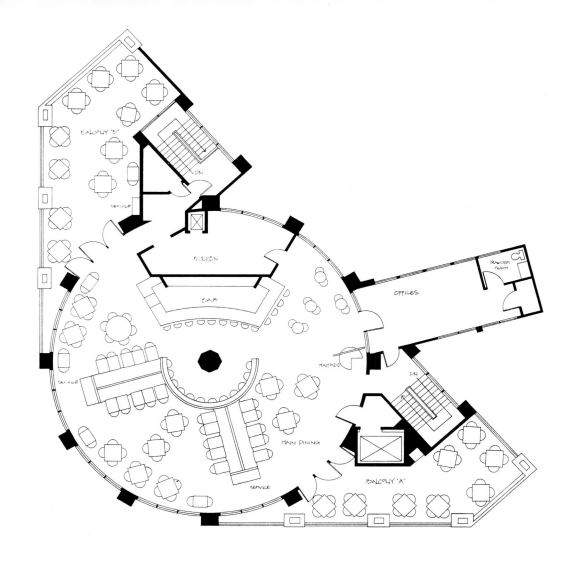

Bistro Bistro

ARCHITECT CHARLES MORRIS MOUNT'S design for this Washington, D.C. area restaurant incorporates the best of both sides of the Atlantic. Modeled after a French bistro, with a strong Italian influence, the simplicity of design and casual atmosphere are distinctly American. The restaurant is symmetrically arranged around a long corridor, forming a central arcade under a series of arches. To the left of the corridor is the main dining room; to the right is the bar. A portion of the dining area toward the rear of the restaurant is raised two steps and carpeted, to create a separate, more intimate space.

The bistro carries many references to classical Italian art and architecture, often used in whimsical ways. Portions of Michelangelo's figures from the Sistine chapel are painted on canvas and installed as murals above the bar and dining room. The scale of these reproductions looks slightly oversized; they act as a light-hearted reference rather than a literal adaptation. The bar itself, painted a rich dark green accented by mahogany, incorporates the balance and symmetry of classical Italian architecture, but sidesteps austerity with its casual arrangement of café tables and chairs. Mount painted the walls of the bistro in soft tones of terracotta and peach, using a rag-rolled faux finish. Bistro Bistro projects a down-to-earth classicism.

Architecture/Interior Design
Charles Morris Mount
Proprietor
Mark Caraluzzi
Photography
Ken Wyner

Type
Euro/American Bistro
Size
5,000 sq. ft.
Seating
172
Opened
1988
Budget
$450,000

Bix

BIX, A JAZZY SUPPER CLUB IN A BACK alley of San Francisco's financial district, occupies an historic building dating from the Gold Rush era. While architects Michael Guthrie and Daniel Friedlander took many of their design cues from the Art Deco style, they conceived the restaurant as a collage. "With Bix," Guthrie explains, "we mix up different styles to create something with more impact." The architect points to the '20s-designed Italian lighting fixtures over the bar, which hang from ornate Victorian plasterwork on the ceiling. Behind the bar, a contemporary mural by architect Mindy Lehrman is an idealized vision of a night at Bix, complete with jazz band and a crowded dance floor.

The interior of Bix exudes an air of opulence and character, which Guthrie says was achieved on a relatively modest budget. The architects painted the walls with silver aircraft paint, which was then washed with a transparent ochre to create the impression of "50 years of cigar smoke." An imitation skylight is fabricated from sheet mica, commonly used in the 1930s. Mezzanine booths are upholstered in a Clarence House fabric designed in the '20s by Walter Gropius, and gain an intimate feeling from the custom wall sconces. A manufacturer of guitar picks supplied the faux-tortoise plexiglass, another resourceful find.

Architecture/Interior Design
Guthrie-Friedlander Architects
Michael Guthrie, Daniel Friedlander, principals
Mural
Mindy Lehrman
Graphic Design
Rod Dyer
Proprietor
Doug Biederbeck
Photography
Peter Kerse

Type
'30s Style Supper Club
Size
2,700 sq. ft.
Seating
90
Opened
1989

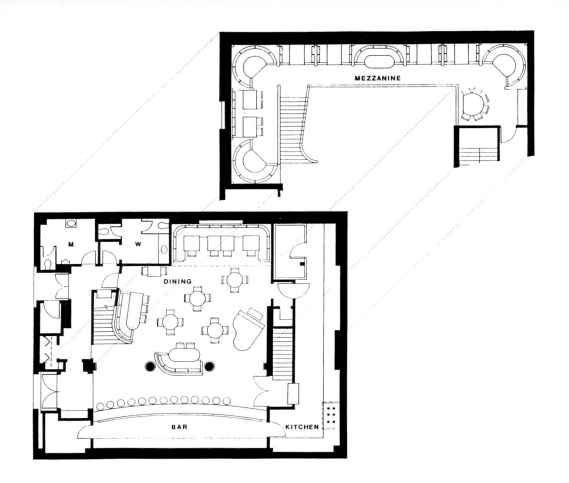

The Black Orchid

THE BLACK ORCHID IS A SOPHISTI-
cated addition to downtown Honolulu's Restaurant Row waterfront
project. Newport Beach designer
Merian Braselle brought an urban savoir-
faire to this island spot, with her use of
rich materials and soft lighting. The restaurant, which is named for one of co-
owner Tom Selleck's favorite episodes of
the T.V. series *Magnum, P.I.*, was designed
to provide for a variety of atmospheres. A
private banquet room was sectioned off
one side of the space, and portions of the
main dining area are hidden behind
etched glass-topped dividers to provide
intimacy.

The interior of The Black Orchid carries
many references to the Art Deco period.
Braselle's interpretation of '30s high-life is
romantic and urbane. Custom etched-glass
panels depict a swingtime orchestra and
dancers, and reproductions of paintings by
Tamara de Lempicka line the entry foyer
and dining areas. The space is punctuated
by sturdy 28″ diameter columns of mahogany. Custom carpeting throughout the restaurant carries a motif that looks both
period and island-inspired.

Architecture
Collaborative 7
Interior Design
Braselle Design Company; Meriam Braselle,
principal
Proprietors
Tom Selleck, Pat Bowlen, Larry Manetti,
Randy Schoch
Photography
David Franzen, Ron Starr

Type
Full-service/Traditional
Size
8,300 sq. ft. inside; 900 sq. ft. outside
Seating
275
Opened
1989

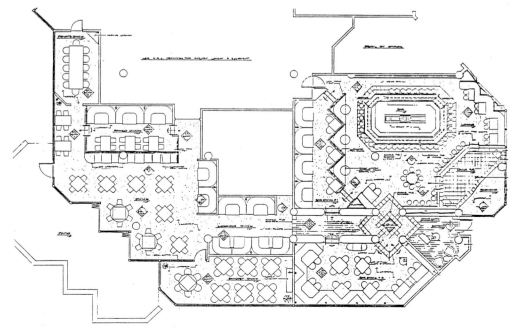

Boomers

BOOMERS IS AN '80S VERSION OF the '50s diner, which architect Charles Morris Mount effectively remodeled from a '70s version of a turn-of the century saloon. The vibrant restaurant in Milford, Connecticut incorporates modern materials and forms that are at home in the midcentury design esthetic, but are immediately recognizable as contemporary. The name refers both to the baby boomer market that Mount's client wanted to address, and to the boomerang motif which the architect uses as a design element throughout the restaurant. The diner, which sits on a busy main road, was designed to attract attention. Mount used neon, glass bricks, perforated steel and ceramic tile to replace wood siding and red brick from the building's former life. The new facade has a sleek but casual look, which is continued in the interior. The ceiling treatments in Boomers are one of the most noteworthy design elements. In the main dining room, a softly curved soffit, outlined in pink and blue neon floats in the middle of the 14-foot high ceiling. The bar and lounge area get similar treatment, with a gigantic pink boomerang hanging over the dance floor. Throughout the restaurant, Mount has mixed futuristic and nostalgic elements for an effect he calls a "forward thrust into the twenty-first century."

Architecture/Interior Design
Silver & Ziskind/Mount
Project Team
Charles Morris Mount, Matt Tager
Consulting Architect
Architectural Concepts, Inc.
Proprietor
Neil Riggione
Photography
Norman McGrath

Type
'50s Diner/Nightclub
Size
7,500 sq. ft.
Seating
120, dining area; 50, bar
Opened
1989

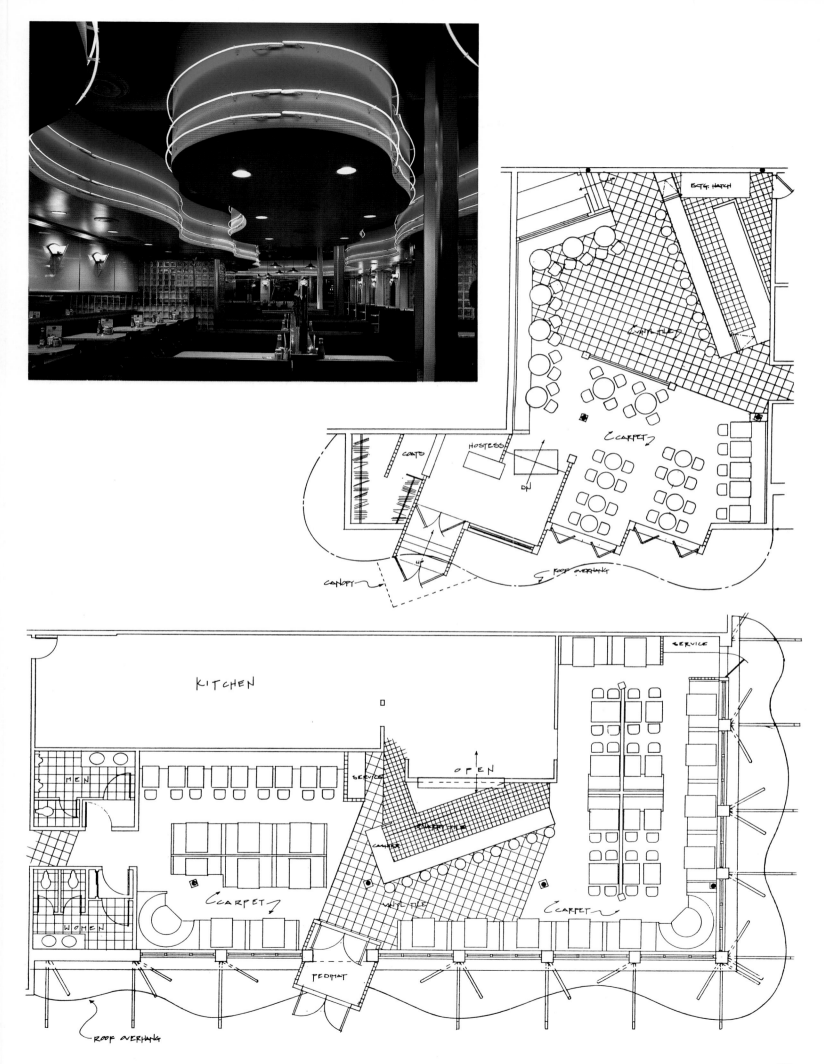

Border Grill 2

BORDER GRILL 2 IS WHERE DINING room meets playroom. This immensely popular Cal-Mex restaurant in Santa Monica interprets a colorful, South-of-the-Border carnival atmosphere with an esthetic that is slightly skewed, highly original and distinctly L.A. Following the success of the original Border Grill on Melrose, the proprietors hired Schweitzer to convert the former site of City of Angels Brewing Co. into a larger restaurant with ample bar seating. Schweitzer's vibrant design scheme was "inspired by the deeply rooted tradition of mural art in Central and South America and reflects a flavor compatible with the food," says the architect.

The interior of Border Grill 2 is dominated by the bold, animated murals by London illustrators Su Huntley and Donna Muir. A series of "cattle guards," orange-painted wood cut into jagged shapes, separates the bar from the dining area and screens the mezzanine and kitchen. Schweitzer installed a freestanding counter near the front of the building which serves as a station for making fresh tortillas and provides a colorful show from the street. The furniture for Border Grill 2 was designed by Schweitzer, and much of it was fabricated in Mexico by local craftsmen.

Architecture/Interior Design
Schweitzer BIM; Josh Schweitzer, principal
Proprietors
Mary Sue Milliken, Susan Feniger,
Barbara McReynolds, Gai Gherardi,
Margo Willits
Murals
Su Huntley and Donna Muir
Photography
Ronald Pollard

Type
California Mexican
Size
6,500 sq. ft.
Seating
120, dining area; 60, bar
Opened
1990

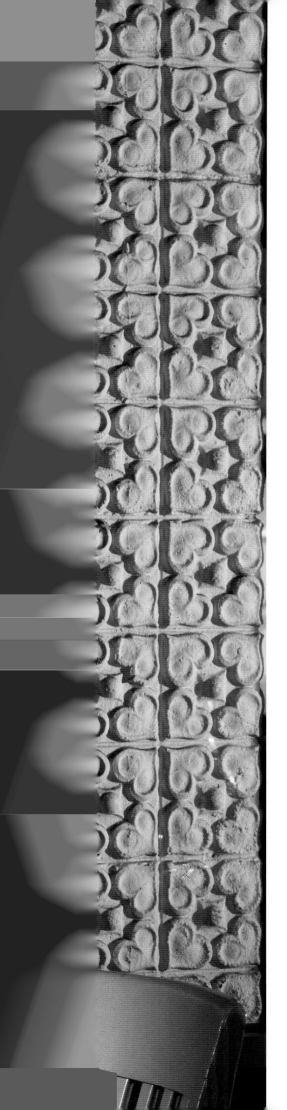

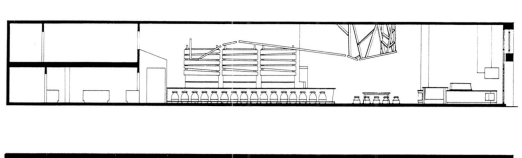

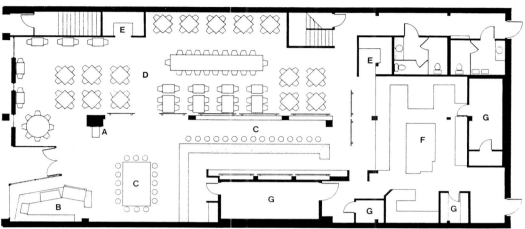

Brandy Ho's On Broadway

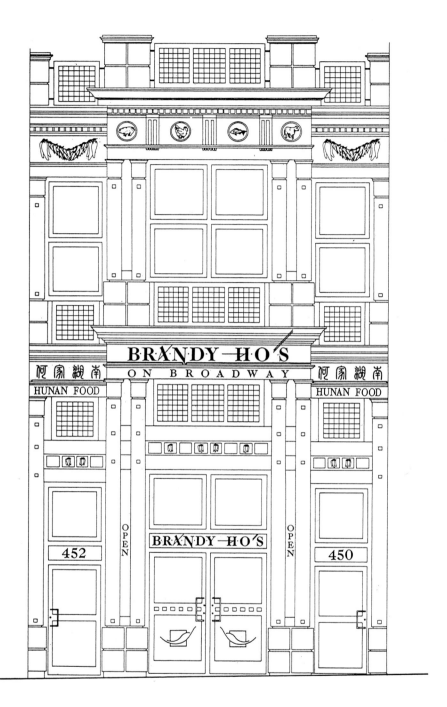

JOHN GOLDMAN'S BRILLIANT DESIGN for Brandy Ho's On Broadway represents a happy marriage of cultural styles. The restaurant's location straddles San Francisco's Chinatown and the Italian district of North Beach, so the architect looked for the common ground between the two cultures' classical architectural styles. "Both employ highly ordered systems in which structure becomes building ornament," says Goldman. The facade of the restaurant, with its red beams and columns, neon signage and symmetrical grid patterns borrows from both traditions, but is distinctly contemporary in flavor.

From the 23-foot high entry foyer, the second level dining area is reached by a flight of stairs that features a red neon handrail. Small, intimate dining spaces are arranged along a central axis, marked out by bright red columns. The display kitchen, which Goldman calls a "brightly lit stage" is seen from a raised dining platform. At the rear of the building, a final dining area looks directly onto a towering rock cliff, viewed through windows and skylights. Brandy Ho's received numerous awards; among them are two for design excellence from ASID and one for neon signage by Neon Neon, from *Signs of the Times* magazine.

Architecture/Interior Design
Goldman Architects; John Goldman, principal
Proprietor
Brandy S.C. Ho
Graphic Design
Ariel Grey
Photography
Jane Lidz

Type
Hunan Chinese
Size
1,800 sq. ft., dining area; 700 sq. ft., service basement
Seating
92
Opened
1989
Budget
$1.5 million, including construction

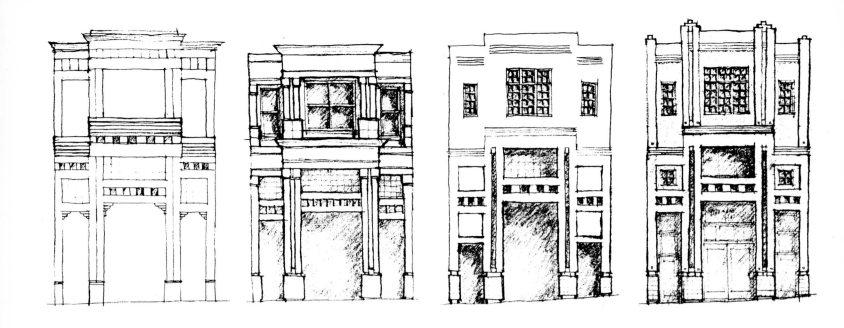

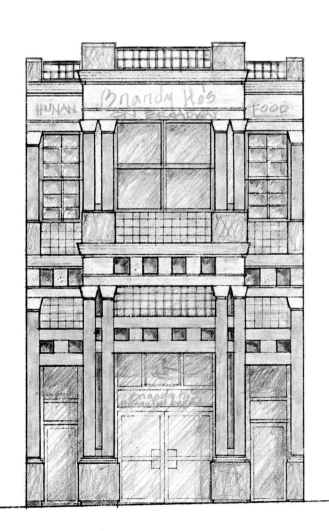

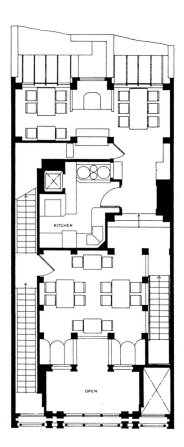

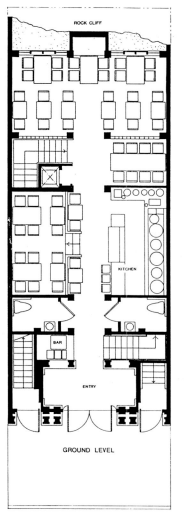

GROUND LEVEL

SECOND LEVEL

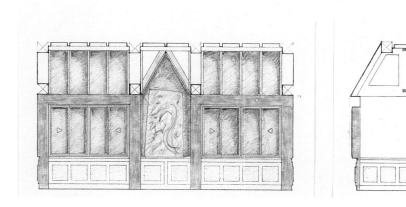

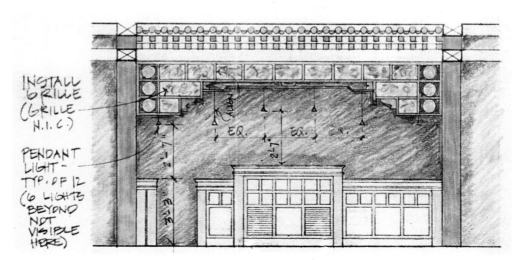

INSTALL
GRILLE
(GRILLE
N.I.C.)

PENDANT
LIGHT-
TYP. OF 12
(6 LIGHTS
BEYOND
NOT
VISIBLE
HERE)

EQ.   EQ.   EQ.

Café Society

A BOLD INTERIOR BY TONY CHI GIVES this restaurant in Manhattan's Flatiron district a streamlined, opulent look, reminiscent of the great Art Deco supper clubs. Proprietor Shelly Abramowitz specified her interest in lighting as a key design element for Café Society; Chi responded by installing 18-foot neon columns, which form a grid throughout the space. These columns cast a warm red glow over the interior and define the modernist character of the restaurant. A 7 foot by 35 foot mural by Gian Carlo Impiglia depicting a '30s nightclub scene adds further reference to Cafe Society's theme.

The main, 6,000 foot dining area creates an "overriding impression of vast space," says Chi. The designer subdivided the room to create "interest and intimacy." Two dining areas with oak strip flooring are raised several steps above the dark black-green terrazzo main floor. A lounge area near the bar is furnished with over-stuffed chairs and settees, upholsteed in dark green velvet. Behind the lounge, a graceful curved staircase leads to a "cube room," used for private parties. The two balcony areas provide seating for 100 and offer a dramatic vantage point for diners.

Architecture/Interior Design
Tony Chi/Albert Chen & Associates
Project Design Team
Tony Chi, Albert Chen, Thelma De Grandi
Mural
Gian Carlo Impiglia
Proprietor
Shelly Abramowitz
Photography
W.H. Rogers III

Type
Cafe/Restaurant
Size
10,000 sq. ft. total; 6,000 sq. ft., dining area
Seating
200, main floor; 100, balcony
Opened
1987

Caffe Esprit

SAN FRANCISCO, CA

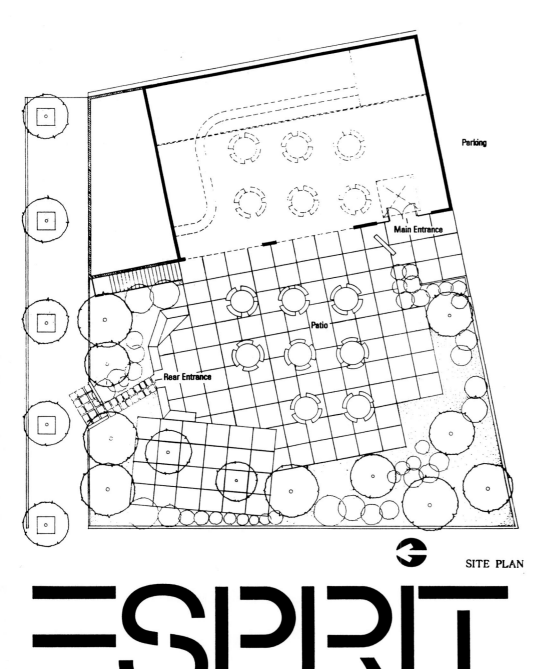

Parking

Main Entrance

Patio

Rear Entrance

SITE PLAN

ESPRIT

THE MENU READS "STYLISH FOOD," and Esprit should know. This casual café, Esprit's first foray into the restaurant business, is located behind the San Francisco-based clothing company's factory outlet store. Originally a grease garage, the space was converted into a popular indoor/outdoor café by Esprit's in-house architect, Bruce Slesinger. One of the design objectives with Caffe Esprit was to provide a functional, stylish environment which was an extension of the company's upbeat, straightforward image. With this in mind, Slesinger used many of the same design materials and elements employed in the Esprit clothing stores, to maintain a consistent esthetic. The spare, high-tech restaurant is filled with natural light which enters through large glass firehouse doors; these can be raised or lowered to open the main dining room to the outdoor patio. The architect installed a mezzanine at the rear of the space, which is connected to the main dining floor by an open steel, curving stairway. Downstairs, an aluminum curvilinear bar separates the kitchen prep area from the dining room. Oversized bleached ash "Alice in Wonderland" pedestal tables and benches provide communal seating; similar tables fill the courtyard. Drew Detsch's landscape design for the patio repeats the geometry of the interior aluminum grid.

Architecture/Interior Design*
Bruce Slesinger
Associated Architects
Gillam/Tavela Architects
Landscape Architect
Drew Detsch
Graphic Design*
Tamotsu Yagi
Proprietors/Chefs
R.L. Fletcher, David McLean
Photography*
Sharon Risedorph

Type
Casual Café, Soda Fountain
Size
3,660 sq. ft.
Seating
100, inside; 50, patio
Opened
1986

*© 1986 Esprit de Corp.

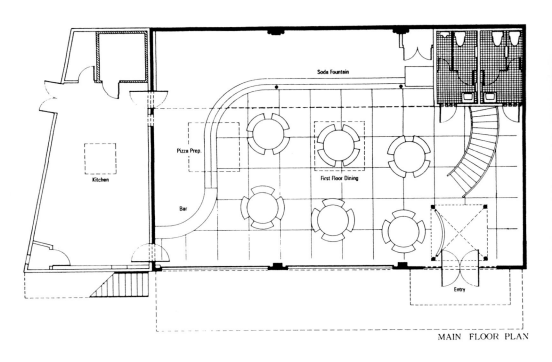

Kitchen

Soda Fountain

Pizza Prep.

First Floor Dining

Bar

Entry

MAIN FLOOR PLAN

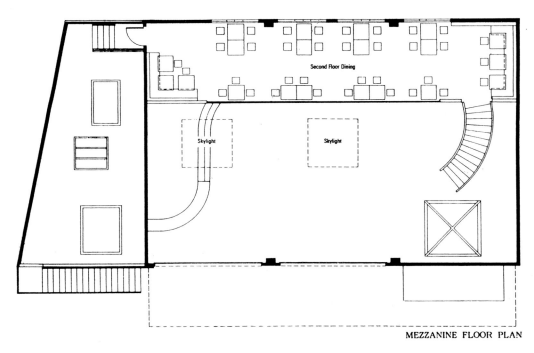

Second Floor Dining

Skylight   Skylight

MEZZANINE FLOOR PLAN

Campanile

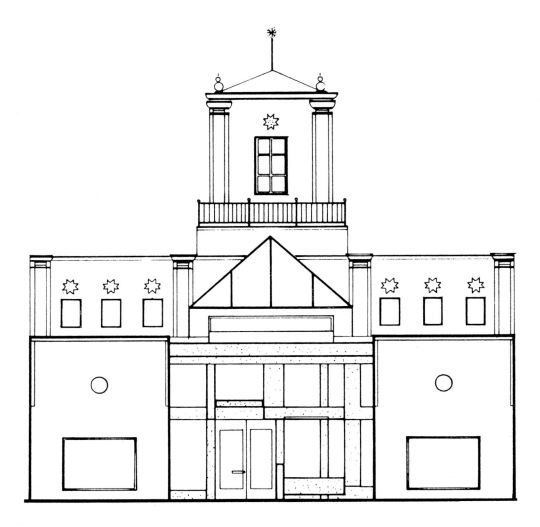

CAMPANILE, A LOS ANGELES RES-
taurant serving Mediterranean-
inspired Tuscan cuisine, is a successful renovation of a landmark
building dating from 1926. Architect Josh
Schweitzer created a cool, modern look
for owners Mark Peel and Nancy Silverton's bistro and its adjoining bakery, while
retaining the charming character of the
original structure. The building, which
once housed Charlie Chaplin's offices, was
one of the first open-air shopping/office
centers in Los Angeles. Campanile—the
word means "bell tower" in Italian, takes
its name from the sheet metal tower ris-
ing above the building.

Schweitzer created two enclosed areas
within the courtyard, one housing a colorful pastel and teak bar, and the other becoming a garden dining area, covered by a
28-foot high glass roof. This skylit terrace
has the air of an Italian village courtyard,
enhanced by its views of the billboard-like
tower. The main dining room indoors is
flanked by a mezzanine on either side,
providing additional seating. Campanile is
both a restrained, sensitive renovation and
a showcase for Schweitzer's fresh, appealing style.

Architecture/Interior Design
Schweitzer BIM;
Project Team
**Josh Schweitzer, principal; Patrick Ousey,
Scott Prentice, Jack Stewart**
Proprietors
Mark Peel and Nancy Silverton
Photography
Tim Street-Porter

Type
California/Rustic Italian
Size
10,000 sq. ft.
Seating
160
Opened
1989

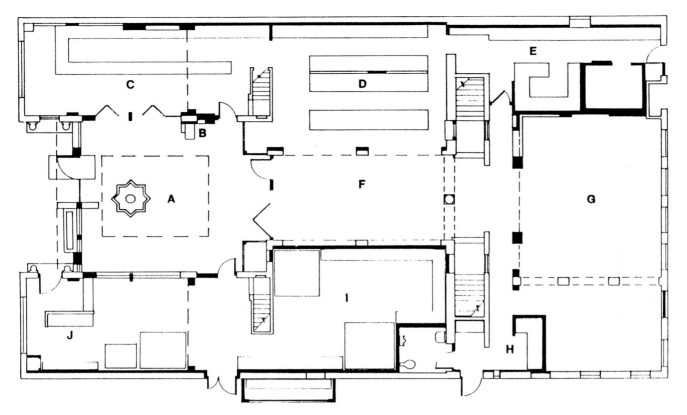

FIRST FLOOR

A. ENTRY COURT
B. HOST STATION
C. BAR
D. KITCHEN
E. PREP AREA

F. GARDEN DINING ROOM
G. MAIN DINING ROOM
H. WAITERS STATION
I. BAKERY KITCHEN
J. BAKERY SALES AREA

SECOND FLOOR

K. OPEN TO BELOW
L. PASTRY KITCHEN
M. MEZZININE DINING ROOM

N. WAITERS STATION
O. STORAGE ROOM
P. OFFICE

Chinois on Main

CHINOIS CAN ALMOST SERVE AS A CASE study for the current wave of restaurant design. Lazaroff's transformation of a rectangular 3,500 square foot former new-wave nightclub into a dramatic, successful restaurant is exemplary by any standards. Through careful planning, an inspired vision and a thorough knowledge of what makes a restaurant work, the designer used every inch to its best advantage, to make a small ungainly space seem graceful, energetic and open. "I wanted to break up the rectangle, so I used curves to animate the space, on the bar, the windows, the artwork and the ceiling treatment." Lazaroff created a "window" to a colorful display of bromeliads and orchids, to further enliven the room.

The exposed kitchen at one end of the restaurant adds depth and warmth, inviting the eye to travel down the length of the room. Lazaroff's color selections of celadon, fuschia and black is her personal interpretation of traditional Chinese pallette. Here, as in the most successful restaurants, all the design elements work together to create a unified image; Lazaroff's attention to detail in the original design for Chinois helped create a restaurant with staying power.

Architectural/Interior/Lighting Design
Barbara Lazaroff,
Imaginings Interior Design, Inc.
Contractor
Pacific Southwest Development, Robert Krumpe
Architectural Ceramics
Mike Payne & Associates
Carpentry
James Douglas Carpentry
Proprietors
Barbara Lazaroff and Wolfgang Puck
Photography
Penny Wolin, Mark Adams

Type
Chinese-French
Size
3,500 sq. ft.
Seating
85
Opened
1984

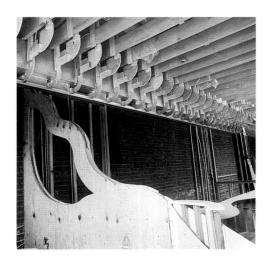

Coyote Café

SANTA FE, NM

THE SOUTHWESTERN STYLE SO POPU-
lar in the '80s is seen at the Coyote Cafe in its original form, and
in its original light. Housed in the
Water Street Plaza shopping arcade in
Santa Fe, Coyote Cafe is several restaurants in one—a main dining area on the
second level of the plaza, a rooftop cantina and a bar which serves lighter fare on
the first level. "We created a voluminous
space in anticipation of a Restaurant/En-
tertainment center," says architect Harry
Daple of the interior of Coyote. The ceilings are 14' and 18' high; large glazed windows facing the street let in the
wonderful natural light of Santa Fe, and
provide a magnet for pedestrians.
Coyote Cafe mixes traditional Santa Fe architecture with a playful take on the region's cultural heritage. Indian and
Mexican motifs are used throughout the
restaurant; murals of dancing skeletons
are inspired by Mexican All Soul's Day, and
an Indian pattern is painted on the adobe
walls. The colors, turquoise, gold and red
are repeated as a tile pattern in the open
kitchen. A ledge above the bar houses
folk-art wooden animals, and animal skins
are used as upholstery for bar chairs. One
of the designers' goals was "to create an
intimate space within a large open room,"
so they sectioned off the dining room into
booth seating, separated from the bar by
an adobe divider.

Architecture/Interior Design
Studio Arquitectura
Project Team
Harry Daple, Stephen Samuelson, principals
Proprietor
Mark Miller
Furnishings
DeWayne Youtts
Photography
Larry Horton

Type
Southwestern
Size
5,000 sq. ft. main restaurant; 2,000 sq. ft.
rooftop cantina; 1,000 sq. ft. Coyote Corral
Seating
105, main restaurant; 90, rooftop cantina; 50,
Coyote Corral
Opened
1984

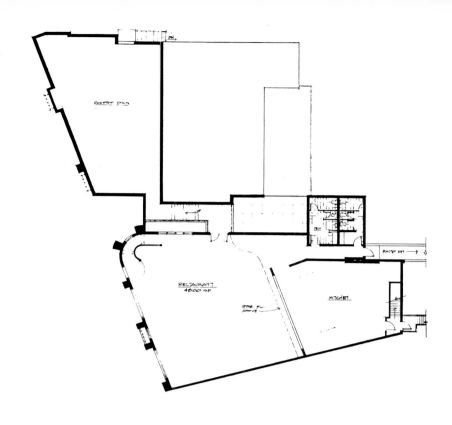

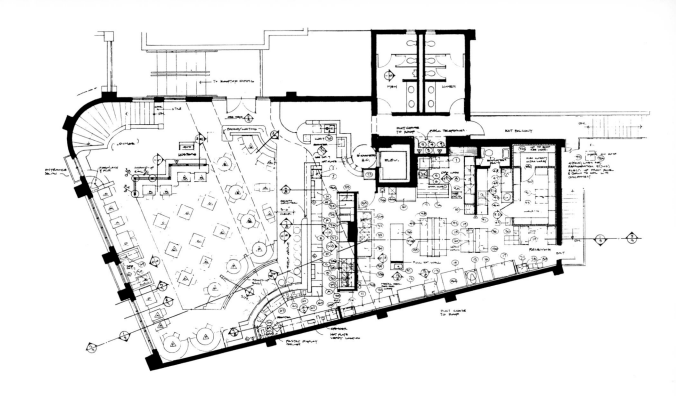

Cucina! Cucina!

CUCINA! CUCINA!
ITALIAN CAFE

THIS PLAYFUL ITALIAN CAFÉ IN BELLE-vue, WA is the work of interior designers Robert Mesher and Joseph Shing. Aiming for a light, informal feeling, the designers used pale tones with vibrant splashes of bright color to sidestep the expected Italian color scheme of red, green and white. The interior, which is sided in natural knotty pine, is brightened by turquoise columns which line the central dining area. Oversized wicker chairs painted the same color lend the room a casual atmosphere.

The entrance to Cucina! Cucina! is appropriately graced with a view of the open kitchen. The designers installed two large wood-burning ovens, which are covered with bright yellow tile to welcome guests and to set an informal tone. A black concrete floor is randomly inlaid with colored terrazzo tiles—a cost effective and esthetically pleasing solution. Cucina! Cucina! is bathed in natural light from the floor-to-ceiling windows on two sides. Additional lighting is provided by ultra-modern fixtures; the most intriguing of these hang under the abstractly painted ceiling in the main dining room. The design scheme for this popular cafe is repeated at several Cucina! Cucina! locations throughout Washington.

Architecture
Curtis Beattie & Associates
Interior Design
Mesher, Shing & Associates
Project Team
Robert Mesher, Joseph Shing
Proprietor
Schwartz Brothers Restaurants
Graphic Design
Tim Girvin Design, Inc.
Photography
Dick Busher

Type
Italian Café
Size
8,000 square feet
Seating
267
Opened
1989
Budget
$1 million

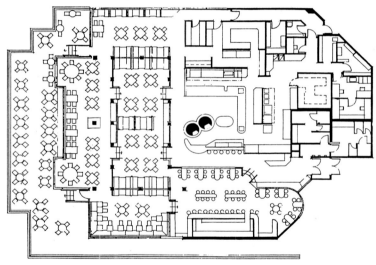

D'Amico Cucina

D'AMICO CUCINA IS ONLY TRADI-
tional in the sense that it is
only Italian. Richard D'Amico
adhered to a thoroughly mod-
ern, Milanese esthetic in his design for
this elegant, relaxed restaurant in downtown Minneapolis' historic Butler Square.
An undisputed hit, D'Amico Cucina was
the first project owned and operated sole-
ly by restaurant consultants D'Amico +
Partners, of which Richard is founder and
president. In his restoration of the former
site of a French country restaurant, the
designer achieved a dynamic, sophisticated atmosphere which he still feels is
the best representation of his work.
"It has a very comfortable, Tuscan villa
type of feeling," says D'Amico of the restaurant that bears his name. Marble-tile
floors and a muted color palette of gray,
peach and teal provide a backdrop for
sleek, contemporary Italian furniture —
black steel tables and Matteo Grassi
leather chairs. The lounge, which D'Amico
opened up to the main dining area, uses
black and white for a dramatic effect,
punctuated by a large faux marble bar.
Framed black and white photographs of
the D'Amico family and their favorite Italian movie stars lend an appealing, personal note to this new type of family
restaurant.

Architecture/Interior Design
D'Amico + Partners, Inc.
Richard D'Amico, principal in charge of design
Proprietor
D'Amico + Partners, Inc.
Graphic Design
Duffy Design Group
Photography
Parallel Productions/Tom Berthiume

Type
Italian
Size
7,500 sq. ft.
Seating
150
Opened
1987
Budget
$140,800

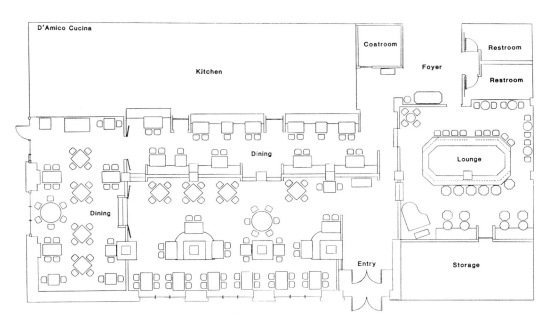

D'Amico Cucina

Kitchen

Coatroom

Foyer

Restroom

Restroom

Dining

Lounge

Dining

Entry

Storage

DC-3

DC-3 IS STARTLING ON A GRAND scale. A restaurant loosely inspired by a museum sculpture studio and located above an aircraft display courtyard, adjacent to a museum of flying could hardly be executed in a small space. Indeed, DC-3, the result of a collaboration between artist Charles Arnoldi and architect Jack Highwart of Solberg + Lowe, fairly exemplifies lofty design. Arnoldi and Highwart chose industrial materials which are occasionally softened by natural elements to meet the monumental proportions of the original space. The Design team effectively partitioned the restaurant into a bar and dining area, which are separated visually and acoustically by a massive glass-filled blond wood grid.

Sculptural shapes serve a function, as in the case of the rusted steel "lunch pail" liquor storage cabinet in the bar area and the freestanding black plaster sphere which forms the entry portal. The restrooms provided another opportunity for experimentation in the form of two linked, jagged ziggurats of stucco-covered wood which occupy the center of the floor.

Architecture
Solberg + Lowe Architects; Jack Highwart,
director of design
Project Manager
Michael McBurnette
Interior Design
Jack Highwart and Charles Arnoldi
Proprietors
Bruce Marder, David Price, August Spier,
William Hufferd
Photography
Tim Street-Porter

Type
Full-service restaurant
Size
13,500 sq. ft., inside; 1,500 sq. ft. terrace
Seating
200, inside; 100, terrace; 40, bar
Opened
1989

Due

I N A CITY OF RELENTLESS VISUAL STIM-ulus, Due Restaurant offers a calm enclave of measured modern design. Charles Gwathmey has created a space that evokes balance and symmetry, through its use of repeated geometric shapes, a luminous color palette and sleek materials. The restaurant occupies a single linear room, which gains the optical illusion of width with a horizontally striped gray and beige inlaid linoleum floor. The eye travels down the room with what Gwathmey calls a "sense of procession." In his design for Due Restaurant, Gwathmey displays orderly wit. He seems to borrow inspiration from classical Japanese design; the grided beige fabric panels and terracotta lattices that cover the walls recall Shoji screens. To open up the room, the ceiling was treated to look like a sky-light, using etched glass panels which are lit from above for a warm am-ber glow. Due has a distinctly modern feeling, characterized by the liberal use of black lacquer and stainless steel for the bar, light and dark gray granite for the ta-bles and by the inventive exterior.

Architecture/Interior Design
Gwathmey, Siegel & Associates Architects;
Project Team
Charles Gwathmey, principal;
Edward Linenschmidt, associate architect,
Jose Coriano, project architect
Proprietors
Maro & Luigi Lusardi
Graphic design
Christine Botta
Photography
Norman McGrath

Type
Full-Service Italian
Size
1,200 sq. ft., dining area; 1,000 sq. ft.,
kitchen/office
Seating
60
Opened
1988

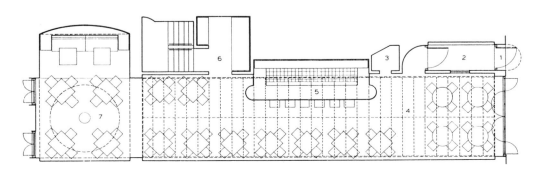

1 - ENTRY
2 - VESTIBULE
3 - COATS
4 - MAIN DINING SPACE
5 - BAR
6 - SERVICE
7 - REAR DINING SPACE

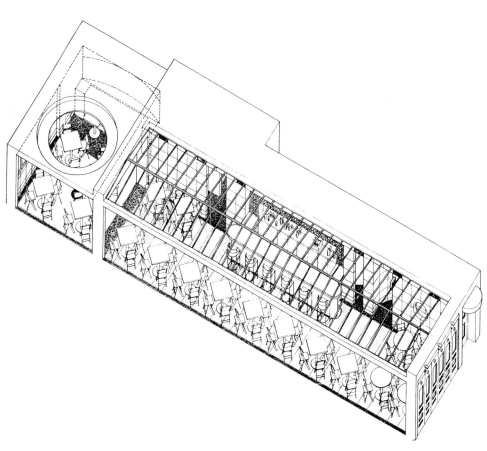

East Coast Restaurant

EAST COAST, A SEAFOOD RESTAURANT in Westport, Connecticut completely redefines the nautical theme, with its innovative sculptural forms and sleek materials. Olvia Demetriou and Theodore Adamstein, interior architects based in Washington D.C., used materials like cold rolled steel, patinated copper, rusted plate metal, weathered wood surfaces and canvas and awning fabrics to refer to aquatic elements, without a hint of the traditional fishnets and boating paraphernalia so commonly associated with seafood restaurants.

Cool blue and sea-green tones are used throughout the 194-person main dining room and the bar/lounge which seats 36, to create the feeling of ocean and water. Adamson & Demetriou came up with a striking "fin" motif: "an evocative form which we used extensively, alluding to the sail, fish fin and boat keel." A "boat ramp" sculpture made of patina treated copper draws the eye into the center of the main dining area, while whimsical "beach cabanas"—teal and yellow striped canvas awnings add punches of color to the room. The one literal reference to the aquatic theme is a custom designed aquarium set into a blue tile wall near the entrance.

Architecture/Interior Design
Adamstein & Demetriou
Project Team
Theodore Adamstein; Olvia Demetriou, principals, Margaret Gaugan and Brian O'Connell, junior designers
Proprietors
Martin Levine, Courtland Williams
Graphic Design
Kelly Allen
Photography
Theodore Adamstein, Jon Jenson

Type
Contemporary Seafood
Size
8,300 sq. ft.
Seating
194, dining area; 36, bar
Opened
1989

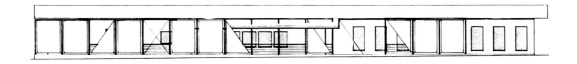

E A S T   C O A S T

EAST COAST

RESTAURANT AND BAR

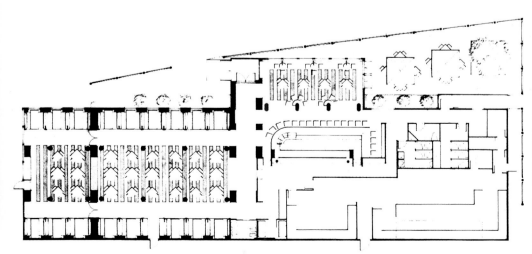

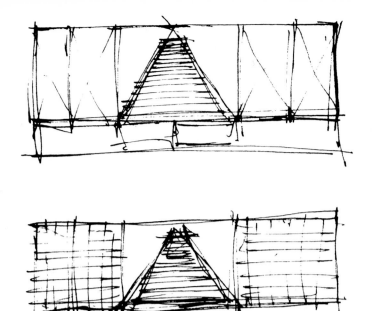
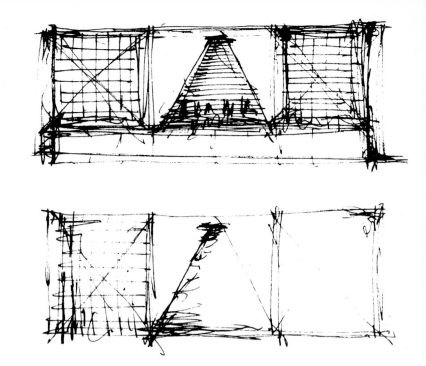

Eureka Restaurant and Brewing Company

LOS ANGELES, CA

"IT'S OUR CONCEPT OF A BREWERY IN the '90s," says Barbara Lazaroff of her design for the popular new restaurant, Eureka, which is housed within a working brewery. Her inspiration came from the films "Metropolis" and Charlie Chaplin's "Modern Times." Lazaroff used interlocking gears, rivets, nuts and bolts throughout the restaurant for a "very mechanized, cybernetic feeling." Her use of materials like hand-hammered metal, copper, brushed stainless steel and perforated pewter continue the industrial theme. Yet for all its metallic drama, Eureka is actually a very warm, intimate space. "It's done on a human scale," explains Lazaroff.

One of Lazaroff's design trademarks is the grand exhibition kitchen, where her husband, chef Wolfgang Puck creates his celebrated California cuisine. For Eureka, Lazaroff also left the brewery exposed, so that diners could "participate in the process" of beermaking. Three gleaming copper brew tanks are visible from the exterior of the building and from the 34-seat bar. A kinetic sculpture hangs on one wall of the restaurant, depicting scenes of Los Angeles, with Eureka as the focal point. Glass bricks used throughout the restaurant are etched with the signature gear motif.

Project/Interior/Lighting Design
Barbara Lazaroff,
Imaginings Interior Design, Inc.
Additional Detail Renderings
Deborah Forbes
Contractor
Pacific Southwest Development,
Robert Krumpe, Steve Magnie,
Wally Woodbury
Architect of Record (Building Shell)
Fields/Silverman + Devereaux Architects,
Peter Devereaux

Metalwork Fabrication
Venice Glass, Ali Harati
Architectural Ceramics
Mike Payne & Associates
Etched Glass Block
Polly Gessel
Proprietors
Los Angeles Brewing Company, Inc.
Photography
Penny Wolin and Toshi Yoshimi

Type
Full-Service Restaurant, Brew-Pub and Charcuterie
Size
8,000 sq. ft., restaurant
Seating
194, dining area; 20, bar
Opened
1990

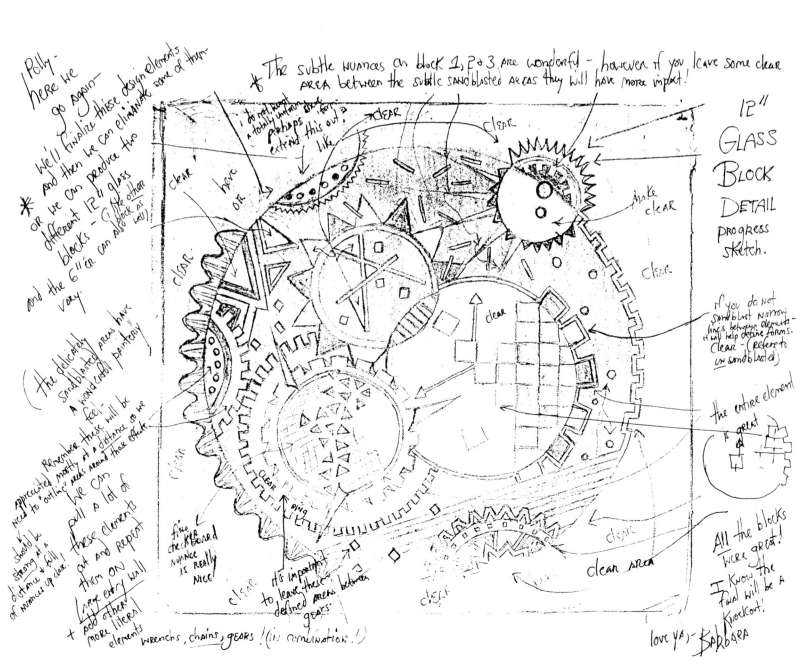

Fama

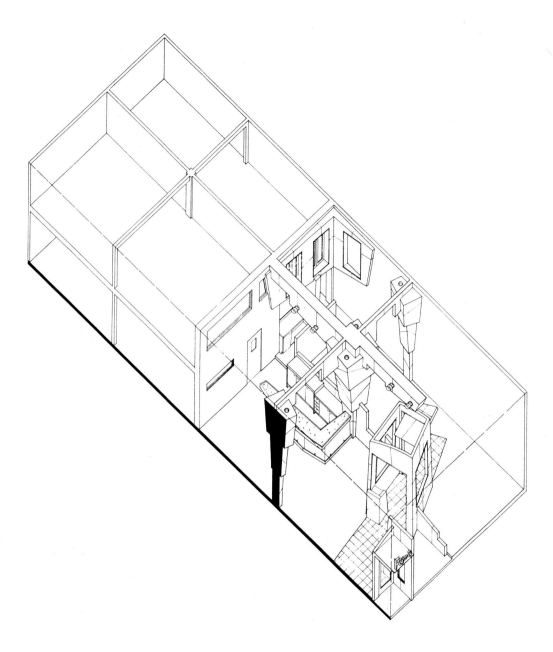

"**A**N URBAN COURTYARD" IS WHAT ARchitect David Kellen calls the stylish restaurant he designed in downtown Santa Monica for clients Hans Rockenwagner and Mary Fama-Rockenwagner. Set behind a transparent glass facade, the interior of the airy Italian café conveys a sense of energy and restraint, with its pale natural wood grains and dynamic abstract shapes. The project was seen as an expression of the owners' personality; Kellen calls the resulting space "both challenging and playful."

Working within a restrictive budget, Kellen devised solutions for the bare storefront room to give it depth and dimension; the former sculptor installed a complex of hollow wooden structures to divide the interior into a series of small, intimate spaces. These natural maple-veneered forms serve a practical function as well, hiding a central weight-bearing column and a clutter of pipes and wiring on the ceiling. A central bar provides seating for single diners, and the private banquet room on the second level is visible through windows cut from plywood. A color pallette of cool neutrals—white and aqua, contribute to Fama's understated chic ambiance.

Architecture/Interior Design
David Kellen Architect
Project Team
David Kellen, Taxiarchis Madouras,
Richard Song
Proprietors
Hans Rockenwagner and
Mary Fama-Rockenwagner
Photography
Tim Street-Porter, David Glomb

Type
Casual Italian café
Size
2,500 sq. ft.
Seating
75
Opened
1990
Budget
$95,000

Hatdance

CHICAGO, IL

THIS MEXICAN RESTAURANT IN CHICAGO exemplifies the soft side of south-of-the-border. Sidestepping the conventional "fiesta" style, Bill Aumiller, principal of Chicago's Aumiller Youngquist, P.C. opted for an understated approach to this 8,500 square-foot space. A white-on-white color scheme is integrated with design elements inspired by Mayan temples and remnants of pre-Columbian civilization. The walls recall stonework found in Central America, while carved wooden snakes decorate the banisters which separate dining areas. Columns spaced throughout the restaurant feature fine line-drawings in the Mexican style. Hatdance has received several awards for its lighting design, which was formulated by Bill Aumiller. "The lighting can make or break a restaurant from the aesthetic standpoint," says Aumiller. He used decorative sconces to provide uplight, and highlighted wall details with spots hidden behind a cove. The architect chose to retain the existing chrome pendant chandeliers, which are integrated into the overall design.

Architecture/Interior Design
Aumiller Youngquist, P.C.;
Project Team
Bill Aumiller, Keith Youngquist, principals
Proprietor
Lettuce Entertain You Enterprises, Inc.
Interior Art
Made in Chicago
Mosaics
Cynthia Weiss
Photography
Steinkamp/Ballogg

Type
Mexican/Central American
Size
8,500 sq. ft.
Seating
215, dining area; 100, bar
Opened
1988

Hunter's Hamburgers

MARINA DEL REY, CA

DESIGNER GINA MUZINGA WAS CHALlenged with creating a café-like atmosphere for this hamburger restaurant in Marina del Rey, CA. Hunter's Hamburgers, which the designer describes as "fresh, bright and sassy," occupies a long, narrow room with table and counter seating, meant to encourage fast turnover. The popular restaurant exudes an air of youthful energy, from its imaginatively painted wall, executed by graffiti-artist Aeryck Faber, to its sculpture of curved sheet metal plates above the serving counter.

Muzingo focused attention on the lighting for Hunters: "daytime light could be natural, but evening light had to be a moodsetter." Wall sconces provide uplight and combat the usual fast-food restaurant fluorescent glow. To engage the attention of Hunter's trendy clientele, the designer installed curved colored neon, snaking through a metal grid on the ceiling; the open ductwork and blacked-out ceiling give the restaurant a futuristic, high-tech atmosphere. Bright red vinyl upholstery adds a punch of color, and a broken-tile mosaic strip around the perimeter of the room is an inventive touch.

Restaurant Design
Muzingo Associates; Gina Muzingo, president
Proprietor
Jeff Sutton
Photography
Peter Malinowski

Type
Contemporary Fast Food
Size
1,174 square feet
Seating
35
Opened
1989

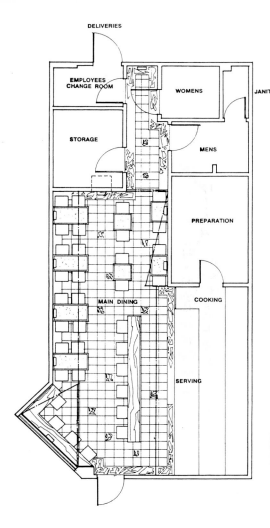

Il Bianco

IL BIANCO

IL BIANCO STANDS OUT AS A LIGHT, fresh haven on an otherwise drab Manhattan streetcorner. The design for this appealing space presented a rare opportunity to Haverson/Rockwell Architects—to create a New York City restaurant with a large outdoor dining area. "The primary design goal was to transform the space into an open and airy restaurant that felt and looked as if it could be located on the Mediterranean," say the architects. Owners Arnold and Bruce Zimberg got an effective and original treatment for their ground-level lobby space in a highrise building.

Haverson/Rockwell opened up the inside dining area by turning three small rooms into one large, U-shaped space. A terrace extending around one side of the building and part of the front provides outdoor seating; tables are sheltered by a large canopy. The architects wanted to "blend the distinction of where outside space ended and the inside space began." They concentrated on lighting design to unify the two environments, and installed large canvas umbrellas, wicker barstools and preserved palm trees to bring the outside in. The distinctive vertical wall sconces in the main dining area, designed by Haverson/Rockwell, are incorporated into Il Bianco's logo, which appears on an exterior wall of the adjacent building.

Architecture/Interior Design
Haverson/Rockwell Architects
Project Team
David S. Rockwell, Jay M. Haverson, principals
Carmen Aguilar, Linda MacArthur
Proprietors
Arnold & Bruce Zimberg
Plantscaping
For The Plants
Photography
Paul Warchol

Type
Mediterranean/Garden
Size
3,500 sq. ft., dining area
Seating
200, inside; 150, terrace
Opened
1988
Budget
$960,000-construction; $1,155,800-furnishings,
$36,000-plantscaping

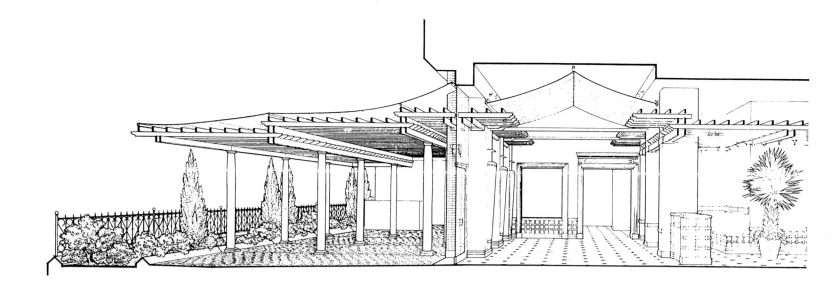

Lascaux

WHEN PAT KULETO WAS ASKED by his client Annette Esser to create a new restaurant in a basement with no windows and low ceilings, he did the only logical thing—turn the space into a cozy, luxurious cave. Named for the region in the South of France that contains some of the earliest known cave paintings, Lascaux serves Basque-inspired peasant cuisine in a setting that is part wine-cellar, part prehistoric fantasy. Stone steps lead from the street level to the downstairs restaurant, where hand-chiseled limestone walls and a mural in the style of the Lascaux cave paintings set the stage.

One of Kuleto's primary concerns in designing for the underground space was to dispel any feeling of claustrophobia. Warm, light wall colors contribute a sense of openness, and wall sconces provide uplighting to blur the confines of the low ceiling; the jet black floor is intended to suggest a void below. An open fire by the cherrywood bar creates a welcoming impression. Kuleto installed booth seating to provide a sense of security and comfort. Lascaux exemplifies the designer's ability to make the most of a seemingly difficult situation, turning obstacles into assets.

Architecture/Interior Design
Kuleto Consulting & Design;
Pat Kuleto, principal
Proprietor
Tourelle Corp.: Annette Esser and
Peter Bedford, principals
Photography
Richard Sexton

Type
Full-Service, Peasant Cuisine
Size
8,000 sq. ft.
Seating
218
Opened
1987
Budget
$2.2 million

McDonald's

A FAST-FOOD RESTAURANT THAT MAKES the customer want to linger is something of a rarity. The McDonald's on 57th Street in New York City, designed by Charles Morris Mount, is almost unrecognizable as a member of the chain that usually boasts golden arches. Eschewing the corporate colors of yellow, red and orange, Mount chose a high-tech, electric blue and fuchsia color palette. Glass bricks, blue tiles and a reflective ceiling give the space a luminous, underwater quality.

Another departure from the fast-food restaurant formula was the installation of a carpet in the seating area, which Mount felt would soften the environment and cut down on noise. The heavily-trafficked main serving area was tiled in a distinctive blue pattern. Easy maintenance of the tiled area, which must be mopped frequently, was ensured by the installation of a slate ribbon between the carpeted and tiled area. The ribbon protects the carpet and also visually defines the curving border between the two floor treatments. The cost per square foot for this project was reportedly no more than a standard McDonald's.

Architecture/Interior Design
Silver & Ziskind/Mount
Project Team
Charles Morris Mount, principal;
Jennifer Wellmann
Proprietor
ISK; Irwin Kruger
Photography
Norman McGrath

Type
Fast-food
Size
5,000 sq. ft.
Seating
175
Opened
1989
Budget
front of house $450,000

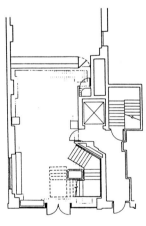

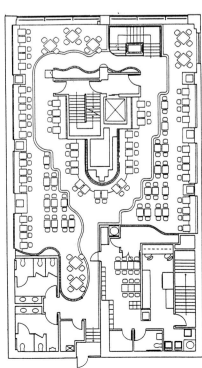

NOT ALL FOOD COURTS ARE CREated equal. The atrium of Manhattan's new World Financial Center, where Minters is located, is a cool, marbled five-story structure that is worlds away from the suburban shopping mall. For Minters, a 900-foot storefront and tropical bar, Tony Chi and Albert Chen wanted to create a lively, intimate space. The goal was to instantly convey a message, catch the eye and draw the customer in, with a fun, lighthearted image. Minters was voted Best Quick-Service Facility by *Restaurant/ Hotel Design International* in 1989.

An eight-foot high trellis tops the freestanding bar, which is furnished with wicker and rattan stools and chairs for a warm, tropical feeling. The storefront itself gets a more streamlined treatment, accomplished with Mike Quon's bold graphics. Metal cutout shapes which suggest ice-cream cone sprinkles are used on the sides of the counter and on the walls to create an animated mood. These graphic elements are complemented by the geometric shapes, checkerboard pattern and stylized illustrations of food items which appear on the menu board. Quon says his graphics are designed to add "life and pizazz to the project, to help complete the image."

Architecture
Cesar Pelli
Restaurant Design
Tony Chi/Albert Chen & Associates
Project Team
Tony Chi, Albert Chen, Elizabeth Errico
Proprietor
R.J. Brown Restaurant Group
Graphic Design
Mike Quon Design
Photography
W.H. Rogers III

Type
Food Court take-out Deli, Bakery and Tropical Bar
Size
900 sq. ft.
Seating
25
Opened
1988

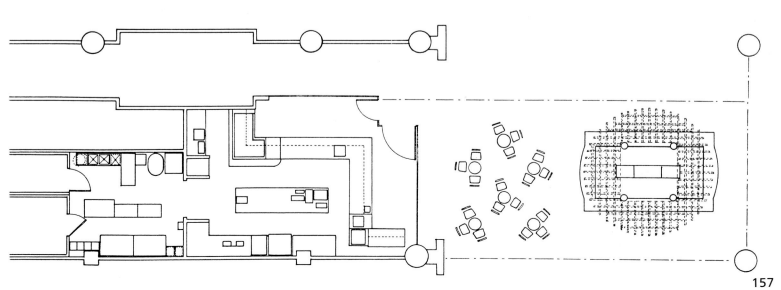

Monsoon

OPERA PLAZA

SAN FRANCISCO

CALIFORNIA 94102

415.441.3232

MARK MACK'S BOLD, COLORFUL renovation of a former Chinese restaurant in San Francisco was achieved with a modest budget and a daring hand. Monsoon displays a "constructivist form," says the architect, based on an "accumulation of new and existing design elements." The large yellow-stained wood structure which announces the restaurant and frames the entry door is repeated inside, defining the bar area. Bright red columns, beams and chairs punctuate the space, modernizing the decor while referring to a traditional Asian esthetic.

One of Mack's design objectives was to provide an environment for both casual, light eating and for more formal meals. The architect divided the space into two zones, defined by a wood and aluminum bench and a low wall. "The slight arc of the bench puts people on display in the bar area, and wraps around the raised dining area like a protective arm," Mack explains. The existing booths in the bar zone were given colored stucco walls, jutting out at irregular angles. Monsoon's artful design is an appropriate setting for Bruce Cost's innovative cuisine.

Architecture/Interior Design
Mack Architects
Project Team
Mark Mack, principal; Mark Jensen, project architect
Proprietors
Douglas Wong, Walter Wong, James Ho
Photography
Richard Barnes

Type
Southeast Asian
Size
3,000 sq. ft.
Seating
160, dining area; 50, bar
Opened
1989
Budget
$120,000, including furniture

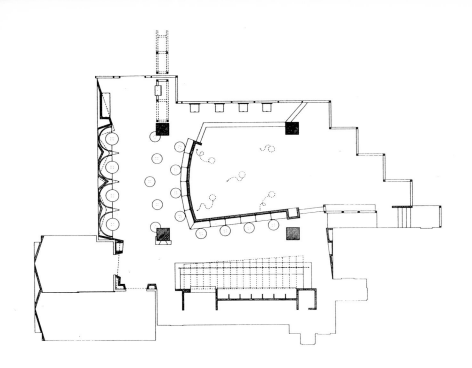

Mulholland Drive Café

A NOSTALGIC VIEW OF LOS ANGELES in more innocent times provided the inspiration for this popular Manhattan restaurant. Architects David Rockwell and Jay Haverson set the stage with a large mural depicting a panoramic view of the lights of L.A., as they might have appeared from the convertible on lovers' lane in the 1950s. The simply designed interior projects a homey retro feeling; stainless steel barstools and black and yellow tiles recall the classic diner, while pastel-painted wooden chairs with cheery red vinyl upholstery might have been borrowed from a midcentury kitchen. Even the floral design—plain red carnations in generic vases, looks wholesome and uncomplicated.

Haverson/Rockwell cleared out what had previously been a cluttered French restaurant, leaving intact the columns and partial dividers which delineated the dining area. French doors at the entrance were replaced with plate glass, and topped with a striped awning and the restaurant's logo in red neon. A creative paint job, in the pale tones associated with Southern California, brightened the room and added to its spacious feeling. Inexpensive materials like tin ceiling panels and standard brass rails were selected with an eye for economy and appropriateness—Mulholland Drive Café's easy design scheme supports its unpretentious image.

Architecture/Interior Design
Haverson/Rockwell Architects
Project Team
David S. Rockwell, Jay M. Haverson, principals
Linda MacArthur
Proprietors
Patrick Swayze, Bobby Ochs
Photography
Paul Warchol

Type
Classic California Café
Size
4,000 sq. ft.
Seating
170
Opened
1989
Budget
$150,000

Mulholland Drive
Cafe

1059 Third Avenue
New York, New York
10021

(212) 319-7740

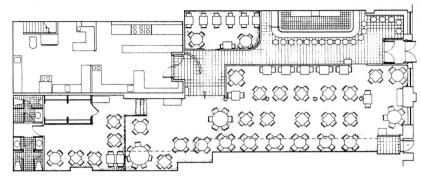

Mulholland Drive Cafe

Noa Noa

THIS STUNNING RESTAURANT IN Beverly Hills exemplifies a new type of restaurant theater, in which imagination supersedes literal reference. Larry Totah's design for Noa Noa—the name means "fragrance" in Polynesian, was inspired by Paul Gaugin's vision of Tahiti, but remains wholly individual in its quirky, innovative mix of materials and shapes. The designer wanted to "create the illusion of the tropics without being too literal." His "fantasy architecture" and furniture design play upon the South Seas theme, while injecting a dose of '50s design whimsy—the starburst ceiling detail in the main dining area and the futuristic shape of the counter seats are a nod to the "googie" midcentury style. The tropical theme is expressed throughout the restaurant in indirect, original ways. Totah used a warm, exotic color scheme, which is offset and modernized by hammered copper and plenty of steel, bent into abstract leaf shapes. At the entry, rough, hand-hewed doors with their jagged bar pattern recall primitive carvings. The custom carpet has a pattern that abstracts ripples of water, and meets a salt/pepper terrazzo border which could represent a sandy beach. On the walls, steel bars form irregular "x" shapes, suggestive of hut construction, and sconces recall shields or masks. Even the bathrooms at Noa Noa display Totah's fantastical design; they feature broken tile mosaics and off-kilter mirrors.

Architecture/Interior Design
Totah Design, Inc., Larry Totah, designer;
Project Team
Lincoln Chung, Noni So and Gus Cornejo;
Bill Townsend, project coordinator;
Ellen Brill, color/materials
Proprietor
Kenji Seki
Graphic Design
Mick Haggerty
Photography
Tim Street-Porter

Type
Pacific/South Seas
Size
4,000 sq. ft.
Seating
106
Opened
1990
Award
Winner of RHDI's 1990 Best of Competition

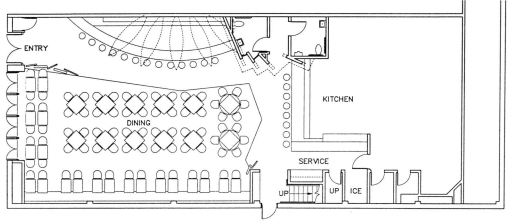

Palio

PALIO, THE MODERN ITALIAN RESTAUrant Michael Graves designed for the Walt Disney World Swan Hotel maintains a strong identity within the 12-story, 615,000 square foot hotel and convention center. The restaurant is deliberately incongruous in theme from the rest of the complex; the hotel is a large-scale pastel seaside fantasy, while Palio displays contemporary chic with bold use of primary colors. The projects are unified by Graves' distinctive style.

"The design was inspired by the food concept created by Wesson—northern Italian cuisine," says Susan Butcher of Graves' design team, who was responsible for the interiors. The firm chose to use the Palio, the annual horse races in Siena, as their point of departure. The traditional flags of the Palio are used as a recurring motif; their graphic stripes, checks and primary color blocks even find their way to wall sconces, tabletop banners and dishes. The russet and green stained wood floor in the main dining area incorporates the checkerboard motif, which is echoed in the quartered-square shape of the chairs. The mural of a Tuscan hill town in the rear dining room was executed by Graves.

Architecture/Interior Design
Michael Graves Architect
Project Team
Michael Graves, principal;
Alan Lapidus, associate architect;
Susan Butcher, interior design.
Photography
Steven Brooke

Type
Northern Italian
Opened
1990

Pappas Grill

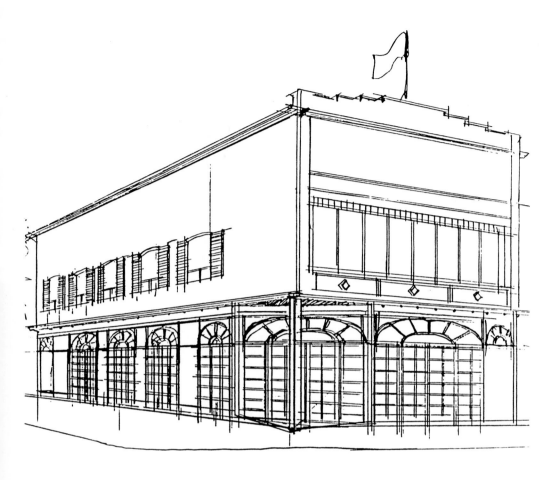

A LONG NARROW FORMER HARDWARE store was transformed into a cheery, open restaurant on Toronto's Danforth Street. Pappas Grill incorporates elements of Greek and French country cuisine and interior design, in an environment which was carefully planned by designer Martin Hirschberg. The restaurant fills three levels, which were each broken into distinct dining areas. The top floor features a lively exhibition kitchen, the main floor a European clay wood-burning oven, and the basement gains appeal through the addition of a wide stairway, a stone fireplace and a large bar.

Hirschberg's design for Pappas Grill "isn't a direct concept replica of any particular place," says the designer. "It simply sets the stage for the feelings and mood of an old world style." Hirschberg and his design team used rustic materials with a light hand; pale woods, terracotta and decorative ceramic tiles complement the old red brick which was retained from the restaurant's previous warehouse incarnation. Throughout the design process, the team aimed for "consistency of design from the basic architectural elements through strong space planning, down to the smallest final detail."

Architecture
Robert Chan Architects
Interior Design
Martin Hirschberg Design Associates
Project Team
Martin Hirschberg, Peter Urbanowicz, Sarah Withey
Proprietors
Tony Kalentzis, William Klianis, George Pinelis, Sam Pinelis
Photography
Frazer Day

Type
Greek/French Mediterranean
Size
5,734 square feet
Seating
200
Opened
1989
Budget
$1.2 million

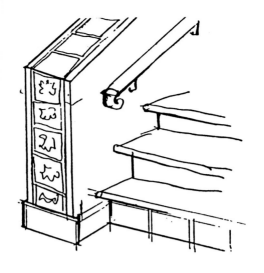

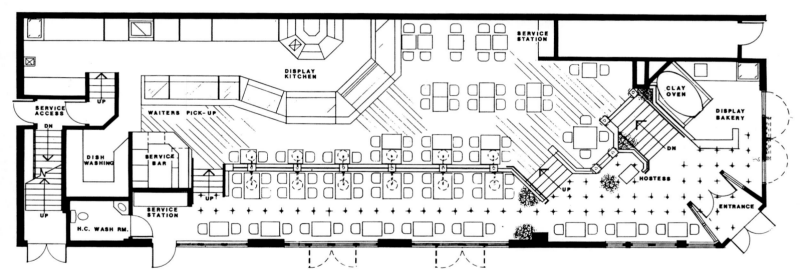

GROUND FLOOR

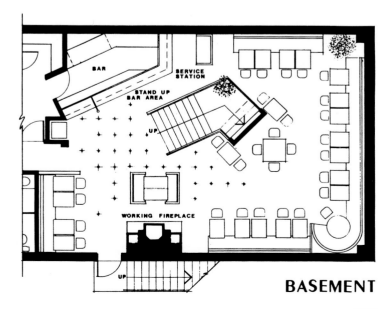

BASEMENT

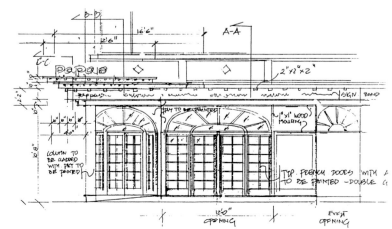

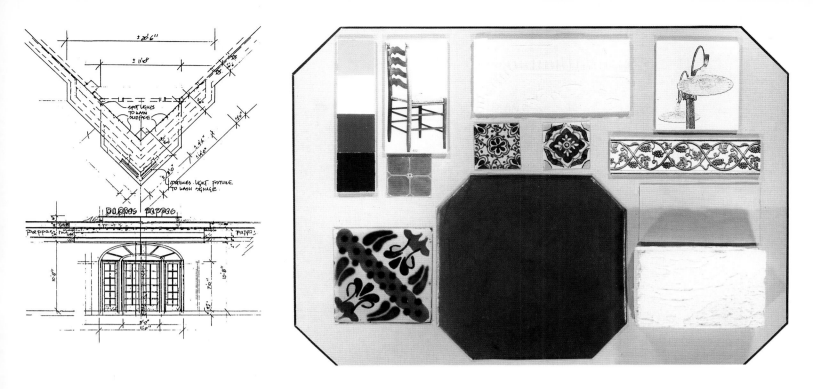

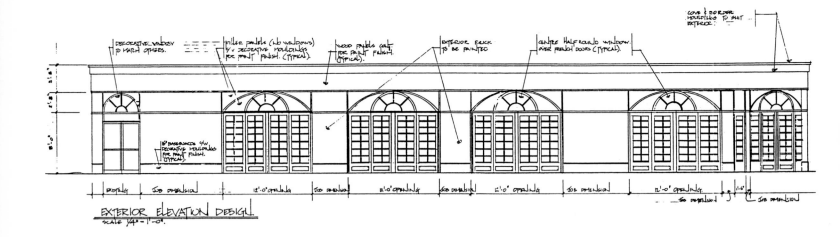

EXTERIOR ELEVATION DESIGN
SCALE 1/4" = 1'-0".

Paradise

GARDENA, CA

PARADISE IS FOUND AT THE INTERSECtion of the two busiest freeways in Los Angeles, an upbeat alternative to roadside dining. The restaurant, designed by Scott Johnson, is an eclectic blend of styles, reflecting the melting-pot nature of Los Angeles. Johnson combined organic materials and nature motifs with the high-tech and kitsch for a humorous and appealing tropical look.

Housed in a dynamically shaped quonsethut style building with a white corrugated shell, Paradise has a softer look inside. The airy space features palm frond carpeting and hanging paper lanterns. On either side of the restaurant, large plate-glass windows look out on lushly planted tropical greenery. An open kitchen and expansive bar bisect the main dining area, and a campy collection of seashells and plastic found objects fill glassed-in aquaria topping the booth partitions. Huge, colorful murals by Santa Monica artist Eva Ohman Benjamin and specially designed handwrought iron chairs by New Orleans designer Mario Villa further define the mood of the restaurant. Even the bathrooms in Paradise carry a touch of tropical whimsy.

Architecture/Interior Design
Johnson Fain and Pereira Associates
Project Team
R. Scott Johnson, principal;
J. Odom Stamps; Margot Alofsin
Proprietor
Andrex Development Co.; Howard Mann,
President
Interior Murals
Eva Ohman Benjamin
Photography
Tim Street-Porter (restaurant images)
Mario Villa (chair design detail)

Type
California Cuisine
Size
8,900 sq. ft.
Opened
1989
Budget
$2,300,000

Patina

LOS ANGELES, CA

PATINA IS A FINELY-CRAFTED STUDY IN refinement. The design for this Los Angeles restaurant is an appropriate setting for chef Joachim Splichal's blend of classic French cuisine and new California technique. Designer Cheryl Brantner has composed a space that is at once spare and luxurious; colors are neutral, finishes are natural and forms are classical in shape. Patina is built on the site of Los Angeles' first French restaurant, which gave the new project a certain "patina of age," says the designer.

Brantner's approach to design is inherently philosophical. She defines her concept for Patina as "a layer of information," which becomes part of the architecture, interior design, furniture design and graphics—all her own work. Patina's logo design, for example, uses nine vertical bars to create an abstraction of a classical moulding; this pattern is repeated in subtle ways throughout the restaurant. Even the striped upholstery in the chairs is an indirect reference to this motif. The exterior of Patina, also deliberately subdued, features four large trellised windows, which "march along the sidewalk," says Brantner; "there's no drawing the line between interior and exterior; it's all interrelated."

Architecture/Interior Design
Brantner Design Associates; Cheryl Brantner
Proprietor
Joachim Splichal
Photography
Tim Street-Porter

Type
Modern French
Size
1,500 sq. ft., dining room/bar; 700 sq. ft., kitchen/service
Seating
100
Opened
1989

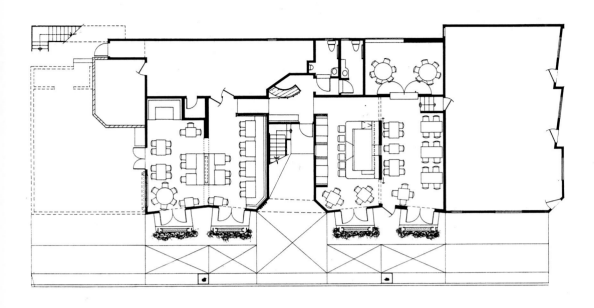

Piatti

PIATTI IN YOUNTVILLE REPRESENTS architect Ron Nunn's pure and simple style. This airy Italian country restaurant in California's wine country is the first Piatti to open; four more restaurants have subsequently opened throughout the state, all of them using the same basic design elements. Nunn transformed a ramshackle building with a false Western front into a light, airy space that lets the food and the people take center stage. A courtyard entrance evokes an Italian garden, welcoming guests into the dining room.

Nunn's solution for the building, which he says was "a simple architectural shape" was to use warm, elemental materials. Mexican floor tiles and stucco walls give the interior a rustic feeling, heightened by the natural wood chairs. Neutral tones are used throughout the space, with punches of color added by the inventive wall graphics by Evans & Brown. An exhibition kitchen provides a sense of warmth and familiarity, and a pizza oven in the dining room reinforces the country theme.

Nunn's well-conceived light touch is a successful formula that travels well; in the case of Piatti, basic is better.

Architecture	Type
Ron Nunn	Informal Country Italian
Interior Design	Size
Ron and Hannah Nunn	3,500 sq. ft.
Proprietor	Seating
Moana Corporation	60
Photography	Opened
Chas McGrath	1988

Red Tomato

RED TOMATO, A COLORFUL ITALIAN restaurant in Chicago's Wrigley Building area, reflects the exuberant personality of its owner, Joe DiVenere. Architect Keith Youngquist, a principal of Aumiller Youngquist, P.C., interpreted the lively mood of southern Italy, Mr. DiVenere's birthplace, in a chic city restaurant. The architect cites the "juxtaposition of country and urban" as a governing design principal. Sleek modern Italian furniture and brightly colored vinyl upholstery contrast with the old world mood created by faux finishes and antique-looking wall treatments.

For twenty years, the Red Tomato's owner operated a takeout pizzeria on the site of the current restaurant. The original wood floors and tin ceiling were retained, although Youngquist gutted the rest of the interior; these older elements add character and interest to the new design. The exterior of the building features a colorful broken ceramic-tile mosaic of floating red tomatoes. Above the doorway, the restaurant's neon logo announces the entrance; the animated "o" from the logo, becomes an abstract drawing of a tomato, and is incorporated as a graphic element throughout the restaurant.

Architecture/Interior Design
Aumiller Youngquist, P.C.;
Keith Youngquist, principal in charge of design;
Jeffrey Everett, project architect
Proprietor
Joe DiVenere
Graphics
Joed Design; Ed Rebek principal
Photography
Steinkamp/Ballogg

Type
Casual Italian
Size
2,200 sq. ft.
Seating
82
Opened
1990

Remi

A VENETIAN FANTASY TO STIR EVEN the most skeptical Italophile, Remi is the first establishment co-owned and operated by the noted restaurant designer Adam Tihany. The original Remi opened in New York and was met with such success, that the designer opened a second location in Santa Monica in 1990. The name means "oars" in Italian—a reference to Venetian gondolas, which is thematically carried throughout the restaurant; in both locations, the windows facing the street are etched with an image of a drunken gondolier, and oars hang crisscrossed from the ceiling. Striped navy and white upholstery fabric is inspired by that used on Venetian gondola seats; this pattern is echoed in the striped light and dark wood floor. Tihany carefully integrated identical design elements into the Santa Monica location, while allowing for different space considerations. The larger New York Remi has room for a fantastic mural by Paulin Paris, which presents a storybook Venice of the Renaissance. Both locations benefit from Murano glass chandeliers, and display a collection of the famous glasswork in the bar area.

Architecture/Interior Design
Adam D. Tihany International
Owners
NY: Adam Tihany, Francesco Antonucci,
LA: Adam Tihany, Francesco Antonucci,
Jivan Tabibian and Claudio Bonotto
Photography
NY: Peter Paige
LA: Toshi Yoshimi

Type
Full-service Northern Italian
Size
NY: 4,870 sq. ft., dining area; 4,702 sq. ft.,
kitchen/service
LA: 2,200 sq. ft. dining area; 2,300 sq. ft.,
kitchen/service
Seating
NY: 172, restaurant; 42, outside
LA: 120, restaurant; 20, outside
Opened
NY: 1987, moved in 1990
LA: 1990

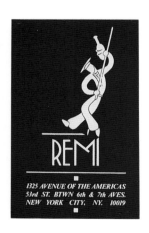

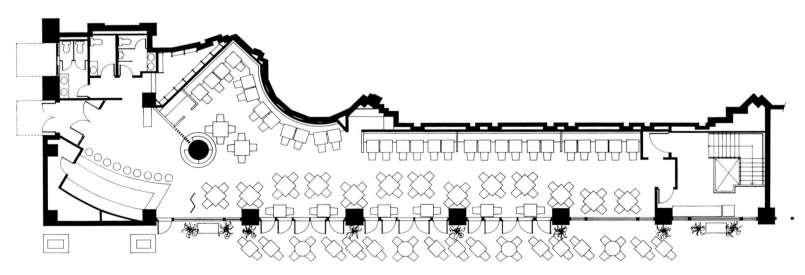

REMI

1451 3rd STREET PROMENADE
SANTA MONICA, CA. 90401

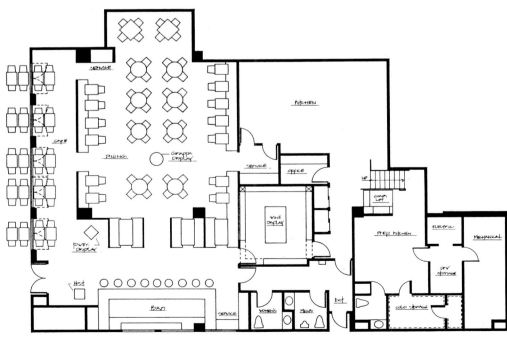

Scoozi!

"**A** TIMEWORN FEELING WITH A CERtain comfort" is how Bill Aumiller describes the ambience of Scoozi! the Chicago Italian restaurant he designed with his partner Keith Youngquist. This isn't a surprising description of a popular dining and drinking spot, except that the design team created this warm, comfortable space in what was originally a 10,000 square foot rustproofing garage. Walls are bathed in terracotta and sepia tones, with age designed right into them; faux plaster cracks, exposed beams, faded frescoes and trompe l'oeil crumbling stonework lend the interior the veneer of antiquity. The ceilings were left their original height, but a series of trussed lattices were used to tighten the space and to suggest a garden setting.

The focal point of the dining room is a 44-foot mahogany bar that seats 100. Behind the bar, colored bottles of varying shape and size fill the facade window, to create an inviting spectacle for the passerby. The exterior itself is dominated by a gigantic red tomato suspended over the door, which is complemented by bright yellow awnings and paintings of popular Italian liquor-bottle labels. "We like the outside of a restaurant to function like a billboard for itself," explains Aumiller.

Architecture/Interior Design
Aumiller Youngquist, P.C.
Project Team
Bill Aumiller, Keith Youngquist, Jordan Mozer,
Trudy Glossberg
Muralist
Made in Chicago
Owners
Lettuce Entertain You Enterprises, Inc.,
Photography
Steinkamp/Ballogg

Type
Italian
Size
10,000 sq. ft.
Seating
325 dining area, 100 bar
Opened
1987

Shane

THIS RESTAURANT IN BEL AIR PACKS A huge amount of whimsy and wit into the little space it has. Designer Barbara Lazaroff took on the project for the owners, who had formerly worked with her husband, chef Wolfgang Puck, and developed imaginative solutions for the small budget and room. The walls were kept light stucco to retain an open feeling, but were hand-finished with silica gel to add pattern and dimension. Bright color splashes of red and turquoise define the theme, along with the black and white cotton upholstery in a "pony" print.

"An open kitchen makes people feel comfortable, makes them feel connected to the food," says Lazaroff. At Shane, the pizza oven, with tilework by Mike Payne Architectural Ceramics, becomes a focal point of the room, with red tile snakes undulating across its surface. The bright tilework on the staircase, also by Mike Payne, leads to mezzanine seating. The existing terracotta floor was inlaid with colored tile in patterns inspired by traditional Indian motifs. Lazaroff's sense of humor is evident in Shane's six-shooting style.

Architectural/Interior Design
Barbara Lazaroff,
Imaginings Interior Design, Inc.
Contractor
Dave Meyers
Architectural Ceramics
Mike Payne & Associates
Proprietors
Michael Kurland, Gerard Izard, Arthur Semler
Photography
Penny Wolin

Type
Casual Southwestern
Size
1,600 sq. ft.
Seating
50
Opened
1988

The Silver Diner

THE SILVER DINER REFINES AND REdefines the classic American eatery. Developer Robert Giaimo, restaurant designer Charles Morris Mount, executive chef Ype Hengst and diner authority Richard J.S. Gutman spent over two years researching the quintessential American restaurant before beginning work on the project. The team wanted to create a truly classic diner, one that would serve businesspeople, families, workers and couples, in an atmosphere that was functional and exciting, but not literally nostalgic. The Silver Diner was conceived as a prototype for a chain of restaurants; construction is now underway for two more locations.

One of the most authentic aspects of The Silver Diner is its mode of construction. The design team opted for a totally prefabricated construction of the freestanding building, which was executed by one of the three remaining diner manufacturing companies in the United States. The design itself is sleek and contemporary, inspired by the streamlined units of the '40s. The exterior features a 26-foot high glass block tower, topped by a neon clock which reads "It's time to dine." Inside, traditional materials like stainless-steel panels, red porcelain-baked enamel trim and glass block tile are enlivened by their contemporary treatment. The intricate mosaic tile floor and black marble counters are notable design details.

Architecture/Interior Design
Silver & Ziskind/Mount
Charles Morris Mount, principal
Proprietor
Robert Giaimo
Photography
Doug Brown

Type
Classic Diner
Size
5,000 sq. ft.
Seating
190
Opened
1989

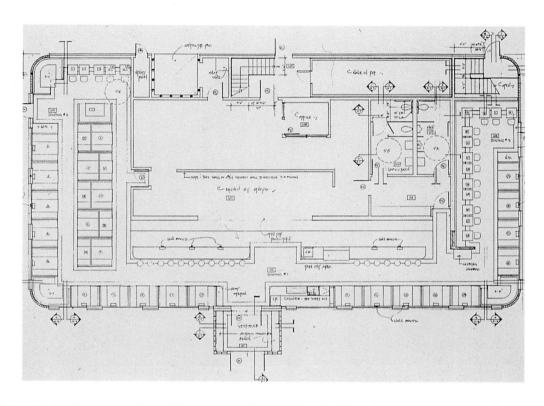

Skipjack's

A SEAFOOD RESTAURANT IN DOWN-town Boston needs more than a fresh catch to bring in the clientele; it needs a fresh design concept. Aumiller Youngquist, P.C., the award-winning Chicago firm, assured the success of the second restaurant in the Skipjack's partnership with a bold approach to the interior. Design elements like a curved bar and undulating room dividers suggest the motion of waves, while aqua blue and salmon pink seating materials and a fishscale motif on the terrazzo floors offer a nautical reference point. Skipjack's is known for its extensive selection of wines, so the architects placed the oversized wine cabinet in a prominent position at the entrance, to greet arriving guests.

Aumiller Youngquist's interiors are recognized for their comfortable, inviting ambience. For Skipjack's, the firm used what they call "warm and recognizable woods" like red oak and mahogany "to create a sense of history." These natural materials are offset by the use of neon, glass block and perforated metal grids. The overall effect, say the architects, "is both exciting and fresh, yet comfortable enough to enjoy lunch or dinner."

Architecture/Interior Design
Aumiller Youngquist, P.C.
Project Team
Bill Aumiller, Keith Youngquist, principals
Proprietors
Chuck Sandner, Jeffrey Senior
Photography
David DuBusc Photography

Type
Seafood
Size
6,000 sq. ft.
Seating
160, dining room; 44, outdoor seating; 35, bar
Opened
1988

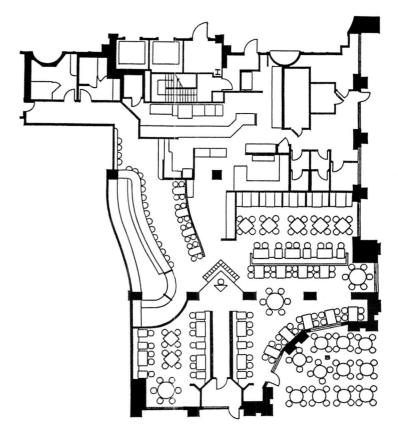

Trattoria dell'Arte

HUMOR, THEATRICALITY AND VIVID color are the hallmarks of Trattoria dell'Arte, Milton Glaser's first solo restaurant project, which he calls an "homage to the art academy." Piqued by memories of his student years at the Accademia in Bologna, Glaser has incorporated many whimsical elements—a looming sculpted nose figures prominently in the front window, and gigantic castings by Jordan Steckel of anatomical details float on the interior walls, alluding to Roman fragments of sculpture. A mural in the main dining room by Theresa Fasolino depicts famous Italian noses.

Color is used dynamically throughout the four separate areas of the restaurant, each one receiving its own scheme of either terracotta, Naples yellow or dark green. Columns decorated with one-inch mosaic tiles punctuate the space, and relate to "scatter rugs" made of the same mosaic tiles, inlaid in the terracotta tile floor. Glaser says that his principal challenge was to maintain a consistent identity that would thematically unify the interior, menu and operations. The designer's attention to detail even found its way to the tabletop, where brightly colored dishware continues the art school esthetic.

Restaurant Design
Milton Glaser, Inc.
Project Team
Milton Glaser, principal; Timothy Higgins, project designer
Design Team
Peter Sebok, Vonee Reneau, Fran Taugmaw, Kathy Sachar
Proprietor
Shelly Fireman
Photography
Peter Mauss/Esto

Type
Contemporary Italian
Size
5,350 sq. ft., main floor and mezzanine; 4,500 sq. ft. below grade
Seating
225, dining room; 60, bar
Opened
1989

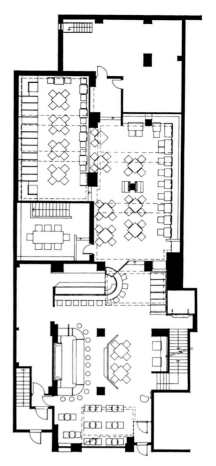

Venue

VENUE BRINGS A SLICE OF COOL California style to the midwest. Los Angeles-based architect Josh Schweitzer's spare, elegant design for the Kansas City eatery serves as a backdrop for the innovative cuisine of Dennis Kaniger. Venue's co-owner Gabrielle Kaniger wanted the restaurant to provide a comfortable environment where people could come dressed in a tuxedo or in casual attire. The architect's solution was an understated modern room with high ceilings and dynamic use of color planes.

Natural light is a key factor in Venue's appeal. Schweitzer used pale tones and natural wood finishes to maintain an open feeling. "I strive for 'stillness' through simplicity," says the architect. At Venue, simplicity takes the form of geometric shapes—rectangular wall panels Schweitzer installed to add interest and dimension. These panels are painted in dusky pastels; the color and shape are echoed in the square, gray-green chairbacks. Even the restaurant's logo uses the square as an integral design element. An upstairs bar at Venue also serves as a gallery to display the works of local artists.

Architecture/Interior Design
Schweitzer BIM; Josh Schweitzer, principal
Proprietors
Dennis & Gabrielle Kaniger
Photography
Hollis Officer

Type
Modern American
Size
2,000 sq. ft.
Seating
50
Opened
1989

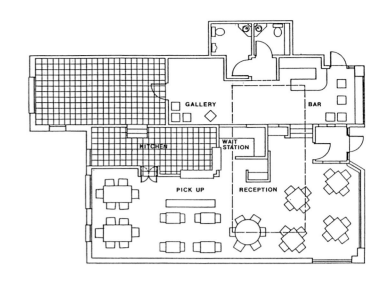

226

Victor Hugo's

LOCATED ON THE SITE OF A RESTAU-rant that flourished during the glamour days of Hollywood, Victor Hugo's is a sleek, elegant space with a contemporary notion of understated chic. The new restaurant, which is named for the site's former playground of the stars, was created from a redesign the space received in the mid-'80s, when it was occupied by Le Triangle. Designer Brent Saville worked to "reassemble pieces from the building's former incarnation;" he started by redividing the floor-plan, to make three spaces out of what had been one.

Occupying two levels, Victor Hugo's main dining room is located on the ground floor, with a door opening onto Beverly Drive. Saville "cut and divided," the restaurant's configuration, placing a banquet room upstairs and moving the main dining area downstairs, where it now shares space with a retail art gallery. Using re-fined, streamlined materials, Saville's design evokes the spare glamour of the Art Deco period without any overt references. A curved bar, constructed of acid-treated zinc and Japanese Tamo ash is a central design feature. The latticework ceiling is softened by floating panels of trans-lucent silvery vinyl, which blunt the room's acoustics and cover exposed service ducts.

Restaurant Design
Saville Design
Project Team
Brent Saville, principal;
Kathy Kerr, project designer;
Pat Whemper and Beth Schnierow, designers
Logo Design
Rod Dyer
Proprietor
Nancy Bergman
Photography
Tom Bonner

Type
Full Service Restaurant
Size
3,200 sq. ft. dining area; 3,200 sq. ft. kitchen, over 3 levels
Seating
200
Opened
1989

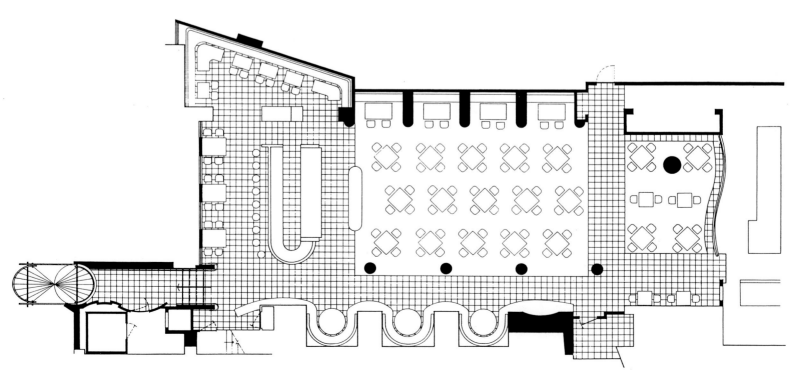

Vucciria

VUCCIRIA, A SMALL BISTRO IN NEW York's SoHo district, transforms a former storefront into a charming evocation of Italy. Architect Tony Chi worked closely with his clients, the Sindoni family, to infuse what he calls a "shoe-box shaped space" with authentic character and visual interest. Chi first installed a central divider of faux marble columns and arches to separate the 1,500 square feet into two separate dining areas. The front portion emulates an outdoor terrazzo setting, while the rear section recalls a traditional Italian dining room.

The Sindoni family, an experienced group of New York restaurateurs, wanted Vucciria to combine the spirit of nearby Little Italy with the artistic savoir-faire of SoHo, without resorting to trendiness or clichés. Chi left a brick wall exposed along one side of the entire restaurant, and painted the rest of the walls a warm mottled gold, to resemble faded plaster. These treatments add a sense of history and authenticity, heightened by the framed antique prints of Palermo, the Sindoni's home town. A low, verdigris-colored balcony that hangs over the "outdoor" section of the restaurant creates a feeling of intimacy, as do the striped yellow awnings that shelter a group of tables.

Architecture/Interior Design
Tony Chi/Albert Chen & Associates
Proprietor
Prinacria Inc./Sindoni family
Photography
W.H. Rogers III

Type
Italian Bistro
Size
1,500 sq. ft.
Seating
70
Opened
1989
Budget
$150,000

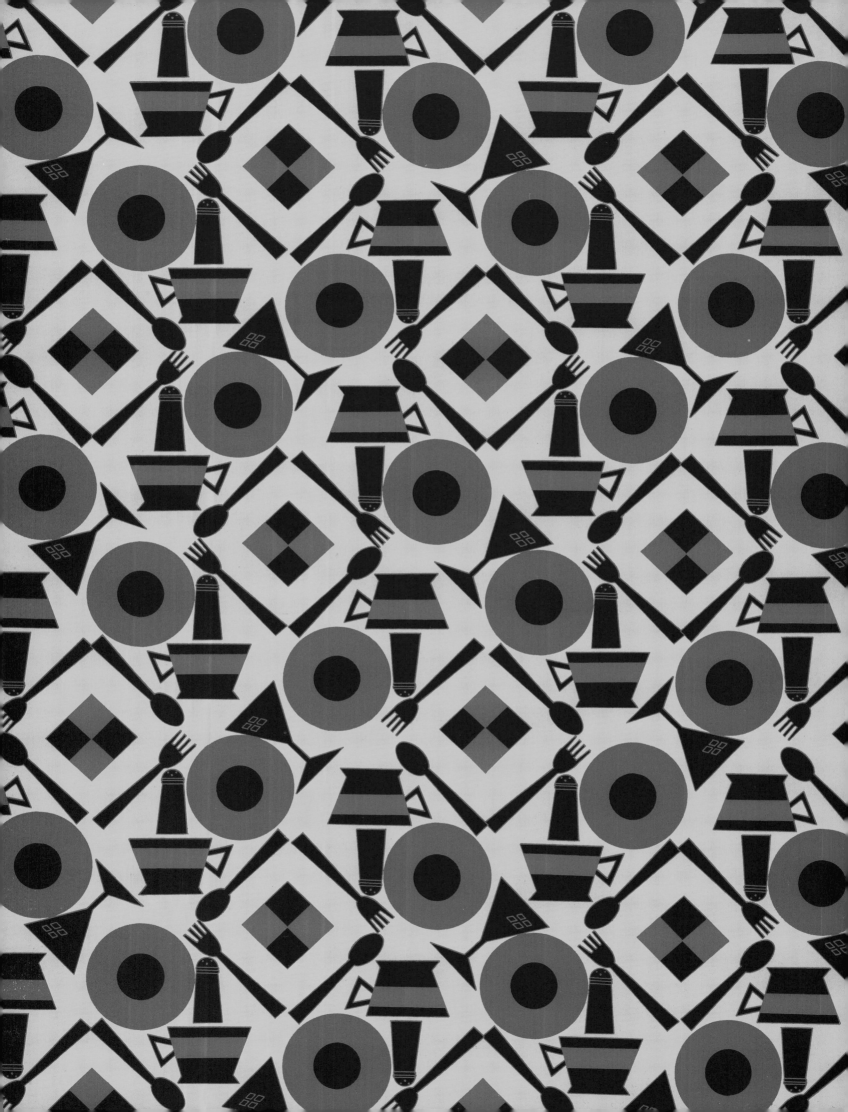

INDEX

Projects

Architecture/Interior Design

Photographers

Proprietors

BIBLIOGRAPHY

Andrews, Coleman. "Best of the West: New Native Food," *Metropolitan Home*, November 1987, p. 141–144

Andrews, Coleman. "Boston Uncommon," *Metropolitan Home*, May 1990, p. 145–152

Bertelsen, Ann. "ASID 1990 Design Excellence Awards: Brandy Ho's," *Northern California Home & Garden*, June 1990, p. 58–59

Bethany, Marilyn. "Adam's Edens," *New York Magazine*, August 1, 1988, p. 34–40

Birney, Dion III. "McGreat," *R/HDI*, June 1989, p 78–79

Casper, Carol. "Skipjack's: A Feast of Seafood," *Restaurant Business*, May 20, 1989, p. 178–182

Cohen, Edie Lee. "Bice," *R/HDI*

Cohen, Edie Lee. "Trattoria dell'Arte," *Interior Design*, June 1989

Eisenberg, Felicia G. "Noa Noa," *'Scape*, June/July 1990, p. 16–18

Eng, Rick. "Ace Cafe," *Designers West*, October 1989, p. 112–113

Eng, Rick. "Black Orchid: Tropical Dining in Honolulu, *Designers West*, October 1989, p. 118–119

Farrell, Kevin. "Style Statements," *Restaurant Business*, July 1, 1990, p. 100–109

Franks, Julia. "Cucina! Cucina! Seattle," *R/HDI*, April 1989, p. 71–72

Franks, Julia. "Urbane Italian," *R/HDI*, March 1989, p. 68–70

Franks, Julia. "Yin & Yang," *R/HDI*, April 1989, p. 64–67

Freiman, Ziva. "Hands-On Hangout," *Progressive Architecture*, September 1989, p. 113–114

Jankowski, Wanda. "Seven Course Serendipity," *Architectural Lighting*, February 1990

King, Carol Soucek. "Chinois: Barbara Lazaroff's Fellini-esque Backdrop," *Designers West*, January 1986, p. 76–81

Lang, Joan M. "Silver Diner: The Real Diner Returns," *Restaurant Business*, April 10, 1990, p. 146–148

Madigan, Mary Jean. "Old World Ease," *R/HDI*, October 1989, p. 70–73

McCabe, Christopher. "Shifting Points of View," *Borderline*, Fall 1989, p. 96–99

McEver, Catherine. "Best Dressed: Monsoon," *SF Magazine*, February 1990, p. 53–54

Moore, Linda Lee. "A Garden of Light," *R/HDI*, February 1989

Moore, Linda Lee. "A Piece of Italy," *R/HDI*, November 1989, p. 60–62

Moore, Linda Lee. "Best Quick-Service Facility; Minters, New York City," *R/HDI* September 1989, 39–41

Moore, Linda Lee. "Honorable Mention, Full Service Restaurant; Brandy Ho's, San Francisco," *R/HDI*, September 1989, p. 66–67

Moore, Linda Lee. "Sea Fare," *R/HDI*, June 1989, p. 71–72

Nesmith, Lynn. "Golden Gateway," *Architecture*, June 1990, p. 78–79

Picard, Maureen. "Timeworn Appeal," *R/HDI*, May 1987

Puzey, Dennis. "The People of Noa Noa," *Inside*, June/July 1990, p. 18–20

Robins, Maureen Picard. "Angelica Kitchen Restaurant," *R/HDI*, September 1989, p. 70–71

Robins, Maureen Picard. "Highlight," *R/HDI*

Robins, Maureen Picard. "Tokyo Roe," *R/HDI*, January 1990, p. 24–26

Rubenstein, Hal. "Chicken by the Sea; Border Grill *Egg*, August 1990, p. 90–92

Ryan, Raymond: "Border Grilling" *Blueprint*, May 1990, p. 31

Sroloff, Deborah. "Cooks in the Belfry: Campanile Restaurant," *Angeles*, December 1989, p. 97, 137

Unknown. "Rum Shack Chic," *Contract*, February 1990, p. 94–97

Weathersby, William Jr. "Industrial Strength," *R/HDI*, November 1989, p. 56–59

Webb, Michael. "Bits and Pieces," *R/HDI*, April 1989, p. 58–60

Webb, Michael. "Deja View," *R/HDI*, June 1989, p. 74–77

Webb, Michael. "Flying High," *R/HDI*, April 1989, p. 51–53

Webb, Michael. "Midas Touch," *R/HDI*, June 1990, p. 65–68

Webb, Michael. "Natural Grain," *R/HDI*, March 1990, p. 36–39

Webb, Michael. "Non Tiki," *LA Style*, August 1990, p. 151–152

Webb, Michael. "Tour de Force," *R/HDI*, June 1990, p. 50–52